Park Ranger

Terry Spangler

outskirts press

Outskirts Press, Inc.
http://www.outskirtspress.com

ISBN: 978-1-9772-3673-9

Cover Photo © 2021 Julie D. Spangler. All rights reserved - used with permission.

Outskirts Press and the "OP" logo are trademarks belonging to Outskirts Press, Inc.

PRINTED IN THE UNITED STATES OF AMERICA

Dedicated to my parents, Dorothy & Wendell Spangler,

who introduced me to Jesus Christ....

and to Wheaton College, which helped to mature me in the Faith....

and, finally, to my wife Julie, who has helped sustain me in it.

TABLE OF CONTENTS

Mt. Wilbur looks down over Swiftcurrent Lake in Glacier National Park.

Introduction

FROM THE TIME that I first visited national parks with my parents as a child, I thought that I wanted to be a national park ranger. When I graduated from high school, I wrote in my personal prophesy that I wanted to work seasonally for the National Park Service as a ranger. This desire was to be delayed by college, graduate school, the U.S. Army, athletic coaching, and summer softball. Intermittent visits to parks, however, kept bringing back that latent desire. The fact that I was teaching high school biology and had my summers free facilitated the possibility.

Finally, in 1979, I applied for a Park Service job. The application required that I rate myself on over 60 skills from 1 to 5, 1 being no experience or education at all in the skill and 5 being an expert in the skill. 4s and 5s required documentation backing up the self-rating. Each skill was then given a certain weight factor depending on the needs of each park area. For instance, an ability to speak Spanish would be given much more weight in a southwestern park than in one in the north. Each applicant was then given a score for each park. This score was on a 1 - 100 scale. Bonus points could also be given (e.g. 5 points for a military veteran and 10 points for a disabled veteran). (Much of this hiring system still applies, by the way.) At that time we could only apply to two park areas per season.

One of the parks I applied to was Glacier National Park in Montana. Even with my 5-point veterans' bonus, my score wasn't high enough to receive a job offer. (I later found out that had I done a better job of filling out my application, I would have stood a much better chance of receiving a job offer.) The only other option that was open was to try for a VIP (Volunteer-in-Parks) position. With the help of Donna Davis from the Denver Regional Office, I began to pursue that option. Volunteers at that time got subsistence pay of $50.00 per month and free housing. As a school teacher being paid in 12 monthly increments, this was financially feasible for me. At least it was a way to get my foot in the door.

At first, it looked like I might be headed for Fort Laramie National Historical Site as a volunteer. This sounded fine as I am interested in American history. Then a volunteer position became available at Glacier, and I jumped at the chance. The position was as a naturalist in the Many Glacier Sub-district. Thus, my seasonal Park Service career was about to begin.

GLACIER NATIONAL PARK - 1979

GLACIER NATIONAL PARK lies in the northwest corner of Montana and covers over a million acres of some of the most spectacular Rocky Mountain scenery imaginable - so much so that it is sometimes called 'the crown of the continent'. It consists of about 75 miles of rugged territory north to south and 50 miles east to west. For a biologist like myself, it is particularly noteworthy that all of the predators present before the European settlement of the continent are still there. This made the assignment particularly intriguing to me.

My first season at Glacier was more one of learning rather than earning. In addition to required training, I went to all of the voluntary training that I could, even on my own time, to learn as much about the park and its operation as possible. In this way, I would hopefully become 'custom-designed' for the park. I hoped that this would result in my resume the next summer being improved enough so that I could be hired as a full-fledged ranger.

I was working in the Many Glacier sub-district which maintained a station log in which all personnel were required to sign in and out and record each of their working day activities. This is the best system that I have encountered in the Park Service to keep all personnel up to date on what is going on in their area of operation and in the park as a whole. We worked on a 5-day duty week and on our last duty day of the week we signed out and signed back in when we came back on duty. The first thing that I would do when coming on after 2 days off would be to read the log from my sign-out time to the present time to update myself on all happenings while I was gone . My first ever entry occurred at 0900 hours on Sunday, 24 June, and simply stated "Spangler - Swiftcurrent Boat-Hike". This reflected one of my main duties for the summer - leading a tour of Swiftcurrent Lake followed by a short ¼ mile hike to Josephine Lake. From there another boat took us across Josephine to the Grinnell Lake Trail for a 1 ½ mile hike to Grinnell Lake. I would talk to the folks the whole way and everyone could then retrace their steps back either with me or on their own.

The scenery along the way is spectacular as so many places in Glacier are. On that one half-day trip, visitors can see glaciated lakes, a mountain stream, a waterfall, several glaciers, and a rugged mountain backdrop. The scene from the eastern end of Josephine Lake is a particular favorite with photographers and adorns the walls of numerous doctors' offices and other places as well. Perhaps the most dramatic event of the summer occurred along the Grinnell Lake Trail, but more on that later.

One of the best ways to learn how to conduct interpretive hikes and to learn about the park is to 'shadow' experienced rangers on their hikes. I was blessed to have some excellent ones to shadow at Many Glacier such as Bob Schuster and Dave Casteel. I learned much from them and the others there. One of these 'shadow' trips was a trail ride to Cracker Lake led by Dave Casteel. I rode along and spent about 5 hours in the saddle as a result - the only horse ride I was ever to take in the park. Horsemanship has never been one of my strong suits! One thing I still greatly regret about that trip was when Casteel graciously agreed to take my picture while I was mounted. Just as he dismounted to take the picture, his horse bolted, and he wrenched his knee creating a chronic and permanent knee problem, all because of his courteous gesture to me.

We also were given regular 'backcountry' days where, alone or with companions, we could explore the park on our own. Many of us supplemented those on our days off. There are over 700 miles of hiking trails in Glacier, and it is important to learn about them in order to pass that information along to prospective backcountry users. Another purpose of backcountry time is to supplement backcountry personnel in providing an NPS presence to contact visitors. These trips also aid in noting such things as unsafe trail conditions, avalanche danger, fresh bear sign, or needed trail or campground repair - all to be noted in the station log.

Another task that all Many Glacier rangers took turns sharing was manning the ranger station. This included a variety of duties such as answering the phone and radio, dispatching for emergencies, giving out various permits, and providing information to visitors.

One of the highlights of the summer occurred on 6 July when I was sent to Bob Frausen's snow school. This training was conducted at a place called Lunch Creek above Going-to-the-Sun Road in the central part of the park. In this training, we learned how to travel safely across ice and snow using an ice ax and crampons (spiked attachments on your boots that enhance friction on ice and snow). Bob was an iconic figure in the Park Service that I hear tell had turned down park superintendent positions because he didn't want to give up field work. He had a background of special forces type duty while in the military during World War II. The training area was a snow bank that ran steeply downhill and ended in the rocks. This was a great incentive to learn how to self-arrest oneself when sliding down the slope! We practiced falling in every known position and arresting (stopping) ourselves long before reaching the rocks. We also practiced traveling on this steep, slick surface, including while guiding a stretcher downhill. Bob had intended to use a pretend victim, but I had managed to acquire severe abdominal pain during the training, and so the others were able to put a REAL victim on the stretcher! Nevertheless, I found this to be an extremely worthwhile day-long training session.

Many of the daily activities were not nearly as exciting, however. While in the backcountry, we carried extra toilet paper and, sometimes, lime to service any of the numerous pit toilets that we came across. The tp use is obvious, but the lime is also a necessity to reduce odor. Various critters are attracted to the outhouse smells, particularly when people illegally throw their garbage down the toilet (although I will never fully understand the attraction!), so periodic liming is necessary to reduce that odor. Marmots particularly like to dig their way in and bears occasionally trash the place altogether. (One time I hear tell that a bear actually trapped a lady ranger inside one for a while!) Much routine time is spent answering visitors' questions, such as: Where is the best fishing? ; Where is the nearest restroom? ; What is such and such a trail like? , etc.

Some questions are anything but routine, such as those involving safety. It was (and still is) important for us to give accurate and complete safety information. In order to do that, it is important for us to be knowledgeable on the subject ourselves. In Glacier, this often involves bears, particularly grizzlies, and nowhere are there more grizzlies than in the Many Glacier subdistrict. If people are getting a climbing permit, it is especially important to give them good info since the rock in the park is soft and can be treacherous.

Glacier waters claim more victims than anything, but the conversation always gets around to the bears. They are unpredictable and potentially dangerous, but injuries/fatalities are relatively few. Nevertheless, many visitors opt to take to a portion of the 700 miles of trails and experience nature in ways that can't be done from the pavement. There are about 150 - 250 grizzlies and 600 black bears in the park, so hikers and campers sometimes come across them. All Glacier personnel are given orientation and updates on bears at the beginning of each summer season both for their own benefit and to better inform visitors. For both NPS employees and visitors, most encounters with bears are relatively uneventful - not always, however.

Monday, 23 July began peacefully enough. I was manning the ranger office and everything was quiet, so much so that I sought and received permission to take ½ of a backcountry day that afternoon. I still don't know why I suddenly decided to change into civilian clothes before heading out toward Grinnell Lake. This proved to be a fateful decision that illustrated that God was truly with me that day. As I was hiking along Josephine Lake, I met 2 naturalists coming back from their nature hikes to Grinnell Glacier. They each had a two-way radio and I had none. Since they were traveling together they needed only one, so I borrowed one of theirs. I had gone only a short distance further when I heard this radio call: " 741 - 224 Charlie". (We give the call number we are calling first, followed by our own - in this case road patrolman

Rick Millsap calling the Many Glacier Ranger Station.) "This is 741. Go ahead Rick." 224C: "I have 2 very aggressive grizzlies here." 741: "Are you in a secure position?" 224C: "Negative." I did not put exclamation marks after Rick's statements because he was as cool as the other side of a pillow. He then gave his location as the Grinnell Lake Trail about ¼ mile east of the Oastler Shelter. The Oastler Shelter is by the boat dock at the head of Josephine Lake. It is a rustic 3-sided shelter where visitors can wait for the tour boat in bad weather. I began hustling toward the location as I suspected that I was the closest NPS person to Rick and the incident and, therefore, the first available to provide assistance. As I neared the shelter, I notified sub-district ranger Terry Penttila that I was approaching the area and would close the eastern approach to Grinnell Lake.

Penttila requested, and received, park-wide radio silence - a procedure reserved only for serious emergencies - and a serious emergency it was indeed! As Millsap and Penttila now communicated uninterrupted, it became apparent what a tight fix Rick was in. He had been on a routine backcountry patrol traveling from west to east when he surprised the 2 bears, probably in their day beds. Since grizzlies aren't very social, this was likely a sow and a partly grown cub. At any rate, he somehow managed to light a flare, draw his service revolver, and handle his radio also. (To this day, I don't know how he managed to handle those 3 items with only 2 hands and, also, to do it so quickly!) As he was describing the situation, the larger bear was an arm length, a flare length, and a flame length away from him while the smaller bear circled him. Every time he tried to retreat the big one would lunge and snap at him. All that separated him from the animal was that 30 minute flare!

As I approached the Oastler Shelter, I could see the red smoke from the flare drifting up from the woods a short distance to the west. I reached the shelter just in time to meet the tour boat which was loaded with passengers intent on hiking to Grinnell Lake. As it arrived at the boat dock, I quickly told the driver about the bear emergency and turned the boat around. Alone on the dock, I monitored the continuing radio traffic between Millsap and Penttila while preparing to turn back any hikers coming into the area from the east. Rangers were also rushing to close off all other approaches as well. Rick calmly gave clear descriptions of the animals just in case he would be unable to later.

While this was all happening, the clock was ticking down the minutes as the flare was coming closer and closer to burning out. This brought perhaps the classic quote of the summer as Rick informed Terry, " It's gettin' to be shootin' time!" Millsap had his service Smith & Wesson .357 magnum - a weapon totally inadequate for one grizzly, let alone two. Once a shot was fired everyone knew that any chance for a peaceful resolution would be gone. The animal would either be wounded or dead, and grizzlies do not take kindly to being wounded, not to mention the second bear lurking somewhere in the smoke from the flare. A true moment of 'kill or be killed' had apparently arrived! Penttila then advised, "Try and get a neck shot, Rick."

This was easier said than done with the critter facing him head on. He thought that he might hit a more exposed area and then when the bear hopefully turned to bite at the wound, to fire a second fatal round into the briefly exposed neck.

As I waited to intercept any hikers coming into the area, I heard a single gunshot reverberate across Grinnell Valley - then silence. Someone reported on the radio "Shot fired!" 741 (Penttila) called: "224 Charlie - 741" ....no reply. I could almost feel everyone listening with bated breath. I'm sure that this was especially true for Rick's wife Nancy who had been contacted and was listening at the ranger station. It was an unwritten rule that if a radio call was to be answered it would be acknowledged by the second request. "224 Charlie - 741, come in, Rick." The thought must have crossed the others' minds, as it did mine, that one round was not going to do the trick, and Millsap would have fired more than one....if he could. The silence was again deafening. After what seemed like an eternity, 224 Charlie answered: "I fired a round over the big one's head, and he's headed towards the Oastler Shelter" - good news and bad news for me. I was relieved that Rick was apparently all right but was not looking forward to having an unwelcome guest, or perhaps two, in my lap. (The smaller bear had disappeared completely at this point). Grizzlies can run over 30 mile per hour, so I figured that I had about 30 seconds to react. 224 Alpha (assistant sub-district ranger Roger Shewmake), knowing that I was unarmed, was rushing to my assistance, but the bear(s) was certain to get to me first. At first, I considered climbing on top of the shelter which was about 7 feet high but didn't think that I would be able to deal with approaching campers from there. Remembering that attacking bears would stop to examine dropped packs about 50% of the time, I determined to do that and hope that it bought me the time to run down the dock and jump into the water. I felt that I would be unlikely to be pursued into deep water. Nothing left to do with the remaining seconds … but wait.

To my relief, 224 Bravo (bear management ranger Mark Battin reported that the bear had left the trail and was headed across the valley. I finished this adventure by clearing the trail between the Oastler Shelter and the closure sign/barrier at the Many Glacier Hotel while others were doing the same thing for other parts of that trail system, ever mindful that the second bear was unaccounted for. When we all got back to the station, we eagerly sat and listened as Rick related his story. Not wanting to create a do or die scenario, he decided to risk one round over the animal's head since he wouldn't have time to fire all 6 anyway. Wildlife are not legally hunted in the park and are not normally exposed to the sound of gunfire. The trick worked but the 'griz' didn't run away terrified but merely ambled off grudgingly. At one point he turned and looked back, swatted a log that went flying back at Rick and, in Millsap's own words, seemed to be saying: "Hey buddy, I could have had you any time I wanted you!". How strong are these animals? Rick tried to pick up the log and could barely make it budge! Thus ended my first experience with Glacier's grizzlies.

At Many Glacier we did much of our mountain rescue training at a place called Wilbur Cliffs. There we practiced both ascending and descending (repelling) on ropes. This vertical rock face is only about 50 or 60 feet high, so it is possible to get a lot of repetitions done in a short period of time. Since most of the skill involved in repelling is at the top, a longer decent in training is not really necessary. I am not very mechanical so learning to hook up my climbing harness correctly was my biggest challenge. The next biggest challenge was to trust that equipment and just lay back in space and wait to be caught by the climbing rope which is dynamic and feels like being on the end of a giant rubber band. As you lay back, it feels like you are falling until the rope stops stretching. After that, it is simply a matter of staying perpendicular with the rock wall and walking backwards. (We don't do 'hotdog' repelling with the giant leaps which is hard on both body and equipment.) Ascending is not as traumatic but is simply harder work. Glacier is not a park that draws a lot of technical climbers since the surface there is mostly soft sedimentary rock that does not provide many safe anchor points. The climbers therefore call this 'rotten' rock. Nevertheless, we do get a few climbers and have to be prepared. It is very important to realize your strengths and weaknesses in practicing these skills. Because I have always had problems with mechanical things, I made a point of having someone else check my harness before going 'over the edge'. I worked very hard on this aspect of the job because of this accurately perceived weakness.

Glacier National Park is not named after the couple of dozen glaciers that exist in the park today but because of the fact that the current landscape was carved by glaciers. Nevertheless, the current ones are great attractions for visitors and some are accessible by trail. One such in the Many Glacier Sub-district is Grinnell Glacier, one of the 2 largest ones in the park. At that time, it was about 1 mile long and ½ mile wide, although it has shrunk some since. Regular ranger-led hikes go there and many people go on their own.

Although travel out onto the glacier is hazardous, and therefore discouraged, it is impossible to keep people off all together. Particularly hazardous are the crevasses that open and close imperceptibly as the 500 foot thick body of ice slowly moves downward by gravity. These crevasses (or cracks in the ice) are normally V-shaped and sometimes quite deep. If a person falls in, their life expectancy can be measured in minutes rather than hours even if they survive the initial fall. If they don't die from suffocation at the bottom of the 'V', they will soon die of hypothermia in the icebox-like conditions. Therefore, rescues must be very swift, or they will be body recoveries instead. Sometimes a crevasse may be totally hidden by snow, creating a snow bridge that will not support a person's weight.

As already mentioned, I attended Bob Frausen's snow school earlier in the summer which was general snow and ice travel/rescue training. Now on 4 August, I had the opportunity to do my first glacier rescue training. It is 6.1 miles by trail to Grinnell Glacier with a 1600 foot elevation gain. We each carried packs and rescue gear, so it is a good workout just hiking the

12.2 miles round trip and takes up a good part of the training day. At the edge of the glacier is a well-supplied rescue cache. It is necessary to have equipment already on-site because of the rescue time factor already mentioned. Once there, we must also find a suitable crevasse to practice in. This must always be done from scratch since these cracks in the ice are constantly changing. Fortunately, on that particular day we were able to find one that met our needs. There were 5 of us in the group that day.

The routine that day, as it was most days on the glacier, was to gather the additional equipment that we needed from the rescue cache, rope up and then, with ice axes and crampons, head out to the crevasse. (Crampons are metal attachments to the boots that have spikes on the soles and toes to allow maximum friction on the ice - They are very similar to those worn by telephone linemen.) Once at the glacier, we each took a turn repelling into the crevasse. We would go as far down as we could go and then played victim while the others "rescued" us out. I wasn't sure what to expect repelling down a vertical face of solid ice but was pleasantly surprised to find that it actually proved easier than it was on a rock face. The crampons actually gave more friction than boots on rock. With 5 people that time we each actually got to practice a team rescue 4 times. We also practiced self-rescue in case we ever had an accident ourselves. Using an ice ax and the toe points of the crampons it is possible to dig into the ice and crawl up and out like a fly on the wall. At the end of the day, with a 12.2 mile hike under my belt and a good workout in between, there was a feeling of accomplishment. It was a privilege to have done what few others have done - I had been on and inside a glacier! In a later season there, we had a momentary scare. We were working near the edge of the glacier when it began to shake, and it seemed that we might be cast into the melt lake along with the crumbling edge. It would have been quite a ride, although possibly a fatal one! We quickly moved our exercise to a safer location.

There was also more training than I have already mentioned, including structural fire training at the nearby Many Glacier Hotel. As a VIP interpreter, there was of course, interpretation training, the most instructive of which was the 'shadowing' hikes. This was especially important for the Grinnell Lake Boat/hike which, as already mentioned, I was to be one of the leaders. It was also important to immerse myself in all of the information about the park that I could find so that there were few visitor questions that I had to answer with the dreaded "I don't know". As I acquired more and more training, I was able to pad my resume to hopefully get a full-paid ranger position at Glacier the next summer.

Speaking of the boat/hikes, a few things stand out that summer. One involved the Millsap incident. When Rick used the flares along that trail, he left a patch of red dye on the ground where he faced off with the bears. Right in front of the red patch was an area of trampled down vegetation where the one animal had continually bounced up and down on its front legs while snapping its jaws, both of which they tend to do when agitated. These telltale signs remained there all summer and were often a subject of visitor questions and comments such as, ' That looks like blood!' My answer was, "Yes, it does." and then I moved on without further comment - No use frightening them unnecessarily. These were always large groups, and I have never heard of a bear-caused injury where there were more than 5 people present. My personal belief is that more folks than that simply throw out enough human scent, make enough noise, and in general 'pull enough dominance' to deter attacks since bears would rather avoid us in the first place.

One trip was made up almost entirely of a Japanese tour group, and I had my first experience of talking through an interpreter. Things went relatively smoothly for a while although I had to pause often to allow the interpreter to catch up. As previously mentioned, our custom was to lead the group all the way to Grinnell Lake and then allow them to come back to the boat dock on their own. In explaining the way back, something must have gotten lost in the interpretation because we ended up with Japanese tourists all over the hillsides! All's well that ends well - they somehow all made it back.

The most embarrassing thing that happened to me that summer also happened on a Grinnell trip. There was a stump along the trail big enough to stand on, and I got in the practice of using it in a vain attempt at humor. I would hop up on it and declare that I was running for public office as if I were giving a 'stump' speech. Then I would pause, change my mind and remark that I was "too honest to be a politician". After one of these trips, an article appeared in a local newspaper (the Hungry Horse News) stating that Democratic Senator Sam Nunn from Georgia was on the hike with his family. I didn't know that at the time, but they apparently were good sports about the whole thing even after I had cautioned his wife about picking flowers! They blended right in and were just regular folks!

On the north shore slope of Josephine Lake, just above the boat dock, is an area thick with huckleberry bushes. When the huckleberries are ripe in mid to late summer it is so common to see bears there that it is nick-named "the bear picnic area". Bears, both blacks and grizzlies, just love them (so do I!). We were supposed to record all of our bear sightings that summer and the station log for '79 is just peppered with bear sighting recordings from that area while we were on my Grinnell Lake trip. We might even see them both going and coming as we were leaving or approaching the Josephine dock. This was a particular treat for the visitors!

The last noteworthy incident that I participated in that summer was a search for overdue climbers. They had planned to climb the Iceberg Notch on 14 August, and were expected back at about 1900 (7:00 PM). Early the next morning, two search teams went out to look for them. Bob Adams and Ernie Scherzer headed toward Ptarmigan Tunnel to possibly set up for a helicopter search, if needed. Ken Ward and I moved out toward Iceberg Lake to check out the notch and look for a possible camp site. A complication of this was that the Iceberg/Ptarmigan trail complex was closed due to grizzly activity. Within about 2 hours Adams and Scherzer had located the missing party and escorted them out. All members of the group were O.K.

So ended my first season with the NPS, and, with the training I had received, I was beginning to be custom-designed for Glacier and parks like it. I also learned not to be too humble on my self-evaluation on the application form. It is necessary in this business to be very realistic about one's strengths and weaknesses. In rescue training, for instance, I was fine in learning the physical skills but had problems with the mechanical aspects. For example, I learned repelling rather easily but had more problems remembering knots and setting up my climbing harness. I always had someone else double-check it before going over the edge. The nature of this skill doesn't lend itself to second chances! As I drove back to Illinois, I had reinforced a great lesson to take back to my biology students and track athletes at Pittsfield High School. When you have a weakness in a skill (or subject) that you need to master, you may have to just work harder at it than those folks that find it easier than you. I think that this principle applies to all of us. At any rate, I could now look to next season with the positive hope of becoming a full-fledged ranger.

One post script on the season didn't make it into the station log or a case/incident report. One day off I decided to hike over Piegon Pass and down to the Sun Road by way of Preston Park - a distance of about 17 miles, but I didn't plan very well how to get back from there. The weather was threatening and I began to hitchhike. When I got outside the park, I picked up a ride from 3 young Indians in a pickup truck. They all appeared to be in their late teens or early 20's. (The Blackfoot Reservation borders the park along our eastern boundary.) With no room in the cab, I was left to ride in the back. With the weather, lateness of the day, and my desperation for another ride, I accepted - my mistake! I soon learned that they meant me no good will. They would speed up quickly and then slam on the brakes throwing me around the bed of the truck. Then they went off of the road into an open area and began doing wheelies. I was hanging on for dear life - not a great experience after a 17 mile hike! Fortunately, as they headed back on to the road, they had to pause for an oncoming vehicle, giving me time to jump out. So much for 1979!

Glacier National Park - Unsurpassed Scenery

NPS VIP Terry Spangler doing a crevasse rapell on Grinnell
Glacier during snow & ice training – summer, 1979.

Glacier - 1980

I APPARENTLY DID a better job filling out my application for Glacier for the 1980 summer season, and with all of the training that I had received the previous season, I acquired an offer for a position as a campground ranger at Glacier. I accepted with enthusiasm. This assignment was at the Many Glacier Campground. It involved the mundane duty of collecting fees in the kiosk at the campground entrance. This campground has a unique history, however. In the 1976 season, a young woman was dragged out of her tent only about 100 yards from the ranger station by 2 young grizzlies. She was dead before anyone could assist her. After this tragedy, a 'hard-sided only' restriction was implemented for this campground. Thus, no tents or canvas-sided campers were allowed. The Many Glacier area is a hotbed of grizzly activity, and the developed area is smack dab in the middle of this traditional bear area. If it had been known when the park was founded in 1910 that this was a traditional grizzly feeding and travel area, human development might have been greatly curtailed. Unfortunately, that ship has already sailed. All auto campgrounds in the park are closely monitored to make sure that all food, and anything related to food, is properly stored, and this is an important function in all campgrounds, so this is obviously so at Many Glacier. Although all rangers may lend a hand in this monitoring, it is a primary function of the campground rangers.

All uniformed NPS personnel receive a uniform allowance that mostly or completely covers all required items of clothing. It was great to finally become a full-fledged, officially-uniformed ranger. Starting from scratch, it is sometimes necessary to supplement this allowance with some personal funds. Every new season, however, brings a new clothing allowance. The amount doesn't necessarily remain the same. I have never figured out how the amount is determined. This allowance illustrates one of the problems of the federal government and the mind-set of many government employees. As season bleeds into season, we eventually acquire all of the uniform items that we need while still having allowance left over. The tendency is to then spend the rest of the money on things that are NOT needed. Sometimes it is done to get items that are more useful back home than in the park, and sometimes just because the available funds are there to be spent. I believe that this mind-set is all too prevalent in the federal government. As a political conservative, I strongly believe that this is wrong, even though legal. I must confess, however, that I have sometimes been hypocritical about this. The extra allowance sometimes has seemed like money that was burning a hole in my pocket. In recent seasons, I have assuaged my conscience on this by not using the excess, and by supplying the park in which I was working some of my extra clothing for use by new employees until their clothing order arrived. Don't look for the government as a whole to get over this pocket-burning habit anytime soon!

Although many of the duties of a campground ranger were specific to the position, there were other more general ones. One thing, of many, that was great about Many Glacier was the cross training concept. Because there were not that many of us, we were given training outside of our primary duties, such as fire-fighting, search-and-rescue, back country patrolling, etc. This gave us better response capability in various types of emergencies. It also made each of us better all-around rangers.

Another great thing about Many Glacier that I have not experienced at the other NPS places that I have worked - or at least not to the same extent - was the sense of family. We not only worked together but often ate together and spent recreational time together. We actually enjoyed each other's company. The cross-training helped us to appreciate each other's work. The fact that we were in a fairly isolated location requiring us to all live together on site in close proximity helped also.

As mentioned earlier, we all recorded activities regularly in the station log, and I have relied heavily on it to jog my memory as to events, times, and dates. If the events that I relate seem to indicate that life there was just one thrill after another, this is misleading. Most of what happened was relatively routine. Some of it was even humorous! At 1425 (2:25 PM) on 24 June I made this entry in the log: " It's just as well there was no early campground ranger this morning, since the late ranger was mooned last nite by an aggressive Golden Ager!" Make of this what you will!

Another entry I made on 1 July was the following: " Unusual Incident of the Day: 3 sub adult humans (boys) came in earlier this afternoon and plopped what is commonly called a turd down on the counter and asked for a positive identification. I couldn't identify it but it looked strangely human-like. Cleaned the counter!"

In a more serious vein, shortly after this entry, a fire was reported in room #451 of the Many Glacier Hotel, about a mile down the road from our ranger station. Although quickly extinguished, this reminds me of something that a government fire safety expert told us about this large lodge. He said that if we entered to fight a major blaze, only 3 out of 4 of us would come out alive. The building was one of a series built by the Great Northern Railroad to stimulate visitation to the area. They are mostly wood and therefore susceptible to fires.

On 2 July, we received word at the station that a mountain goat carcass was present along the Ptarmigan Lake Trail. Fire guard Bill Bathke and I were sent out to investigate. Sure enough, the carcass was along the trail near the lake. There were drag marks near the 200 pound carcass. It had been dragged a considerable distance so it was obviously being fed on by something large and strong. We had seen a family of wolverines on the way in, and it could have been them, but it also could have been something bigger, like a grizzly. The area was rocky and devoid of tracks, but we had to assume that it had or would attract grizzlies. We called this information in and the trail was closed.

This action reflects a classic example of Glacier bear management policy. Basically, we consider the backcountry theirs and the front country ours. Thus, if a bear presents a danger in a developed area, the animal is removed (one way or another). If the danger is in the backcountry, the people are normally removed (i.e. by closing the area or trail). Both black bears and grizzlies are omnivores, meaning that they eat both vegetation and meat. In Glacier a grizzly's diet consists of 80-90% vegetation and the rest animal matter. They are not particularly skilled predators, especially when compared to others such as wolves and mountain lions. Thus, they often act as scavengers in driving off more skilled hunters from their kills. Since this is the case, grizzlies tend to more aggressively defend a carcass than they do a vegetation source. So in a situation like that just described, a potentially dangerous man/bear confrontation is avoided by closing the trail.

Once the trail is closed, the normal procedure is to allow the carcass to be consumed before opening the trail again. In order to do this, it must be monitored regularly. In this and other cases, I was one of the poor slobs enlisted to do this. I was not armed in 1980, and bears don't want rangers near their carcasses any more than anyone else! Sometimes the pressure builds to open trails, particularly if the trail is especially popular, or its closure cuts into the concessionaire's profits. Since the Ptarmigan Trail is very popular, it was decided to move the carcass a bit prematurely. In all fairness, there wasn't much meat left on it anyway. Nevertheless, I did a lot of looking over my shoulder as I tied a rope around its neck and dragged it down into the woods - without a climbable tree in sight! Fortunately, everything worked out all right since no bear was around. I was even able to retrieve one of the goat's horns as a souvenir!

The next incident of note occurred on 8 July on what up to that time was a relatively routine afternoon. I was working the information desk in the ranger station when law enforcement ranger Norm Coy answered the phone in the back office. He asked me to take the call yelling,"Terry…phone….emergency!" He quickly headed out the door as his coffee cup rattled and spun on the floor. I quickly picked up the phone. On the other end was the calm voice of fellow campground ranger Bob Adams. He was at the Many Glacier Hotel and said that a 10 year old boy had received a life-threatening cut to his neck. I immediately began dispatching Many Glacier rangers to the scene. The hotel is only about a mile from the station so help arrived quickly with our station wagon ambulance. After the dispatch, I left the phone and radio with other personnel and responded to the hotel to assist. We asked for and received park-wide radio silence to accommodate the emergency. This allowed us to have uninterrupted radio communication for the emergency without being overridden by routine radio traffic.

It turned out that the boy had seen a ground squirrel through what he thought was an open door. As he ran through the "door" to chase the animal, it turned out to be not a door but a floor-length plate glass window. A shard of glass partially severed both a jugular vein and a carotid artery. Bob Adams just happened to be off-duty in the building at the time.… fortunately! He carried the child to the first aid room while applying direct pressure in an attempt to stop the bleeding. Unfortunately, the room was locked and no hotel medical people were on duty at the time. Fire guard Dick Bahr was able to get a plasma IV in, and the youth was being loaded into our ambulance as I arrived. The nearest hospital there is in Cardston, Alberta. Within about an hour from the time that we received the report the ambulance was at the hospital. The blood loss was massive, but the young man survived, having possible nerve damage to the face, however.

I was left to start the post-incident investigation. When I approached the first-aid room, I became aware of just how massive that blood loss was. My shoes sloshed across the blood-soaked carpet. Somehow they got into the room because there was blood spattered on the walls in all directions.

The hotel officials had been urged to put tape on the full-length windows to indicate doors, not windows, but it took this accident to finally get it done. This could have easily been a fatality, but the resiliency of youth, the quick action of our first responders, and the mercy of the Lord made for a better outcome.

The next incident that stands out occurred on 13 July and involved a mountain rescue. All of us were required to have a 'ready pack' with us when on duty so that we could be enroute to a rescue within 5 minutes of notification. In the pack, we would have everything that would be needed to spend an overnight in the mountains, if necessary, with a victim and to minister to them. The normal procedure when notified of a needed rescue would be to send out what is called a hasty party with their ready packs within that 5 minutes. This crew would locate the victim(s) and mark the route to the location with flagging for the primary rescue party to follow. The hasty party begins the rescue setup as well as deal with immediate first aid needs. After sizing up the scene, they radio back precise rescue and EMS equipment needs for this primary rescue party to bring. These items are then brought to the scene from the rescue cache.

In this case, at 0755 hours on the above mentioned date, a fisherman reported seeing a person fall on Grinnell Point above the east end of Josephine Lake. Our fire crew was sent out as the hasty party. I followed as part of the primary rescue party of about a half dozen personnel. This episode ended up as a rescue rather than a recovery, with a good outcome for the victim. We tended to his injuries, placed him in a litter, and repelled him down the mountain. We had him down and out by about 1330 - certainly a relief for his wife and 2 children staying in the Many Glacier Campground!

If you were to read our station log, you would find it curious that a life-death situation might be recorded right next to a totally routine one such as, 'the garbage has not been picked up yet'. This is a perfect illustration of the fact that life goes on, and, that no matter what happens, the regular things need to be taken care of, regardless of the unexpected emergencies that occur.

As mentioned before, in the summer of 1976, 2 young grizzlies dragged a young woman out of her tent in the Many Glacier Campground. This occurred only about a 100 yards from our ranger station. She died before anyone could help her. The Many Glacier Sub-district is a traditional grizzly travel area. After this tragedy, it was decided to make this campground 'hard-sided' only. Thus, tent camping was eliminated and only RV's completely contained in metal or other hard material were allowed. The unintended consequence of this was that backpackers could no longer use the campground as a stop on a back packing trip. The solution to this problem was to build a bear-proof cage for these folks to pitch their tents in. This proved to be a very unpopular solution for people who like the wide-open spaces. This resulted in a humorous sign being posted on the door of the cage on the 20th of July - "PLEASE DO NOT FEED THE HUMANS." There were also complaints that the ground inside the cage was too thorny and too rocky. One colorful comment: "If God cast Satan into Hell, he got as far as the bear enclosure."

Glacier hasn't always been as attentive to bear-related visitor safety. The park was founded in 1910, and, for the first 57 years of its existence, there was not a single documented case of a bear-caused human fatality. Relatively little attention was given to the fact that some of these large omnivores were becoming addicted to human garbage and that some of this garbage was being thrown out indiscriminately. At one location (Granite Park Chalet), it was actually tossed out for the bears in order to entertain visitors. NPS biologists knew that this was a dangerous policy, but the decision makers were thinking reactively instead of preventively and took a 'no harm - no foul' attitude. Grizzlies are very exploratory in their food habits, and on the night of 13-14 August 1967, this was tragically illustrated. On that night in different campgrounds in the park, two 19-year old young women were killed in predatory attacks by two garbage habituated bears. These bears had taken the exploration one step farther - from associating people with food to associating people AS food, and, yes, one of those attacks occurred at Granite Park!

These incidents revolutionized bear management everywhere. In Glacier, after the offending animals were hunted down, important new policies were instituted and enforced. Bear-proof garbage cans were installed, and the garbage was picked up every day. Some trails were permanently closed, and strict food management regulations were established in all campgrounds.

Visitors were informed of these and other new related rules. All of this helped, but only if visitors obeyed them….

In the early morning hours of 25 July, two young concession employees were killed by a grizzly just inside the park along Divide Creek in the St. Mary Sub-district. They were illegally camped right in the middle of a game trail. They were in the wrong place at the wrong time. A board of inquiry was convened to investigate the tragedy, but the bottom line is that not much can be done when people do not follow obvious safety rules. The news media were all over the story. More people, by far, die in Glacier from drowning and other mishaps than from bears, but those stories are not as sensational. People Magazine even showed up and had a featured article. A picture showed up in that magazine that actually showed the back of my head- my only claim to fame! On the same day as the fatality, a hiker fell over Ptarmigan Falls and miraculously walked away with only cuts and bruises. This incident would be expected to be fatal, but it drew little media interest.

During this same time period, we were, ironically, dealing with a chronic bear management issue. People were stealing bear caution signs from our trailheads. The Park SOP was for two signs to always be posted. A green sign was a general caution to backcountry users. A white sign gave special instructions for hiking, camping, and fishing in bear country. If any recent grizzly signs had been noted along a particular trail, an orange warning sign was also posted at the trailhead. This 'grizzly frequenting' sign was a particularly desirable souvenir. All of us were enlisted to monitor the trailhead signs and replace them quickly when they disappeared. We peppered all signs with staple guns so they would be difficult to remove intact, but they sometimes disappeared anyway. Even though a warning appeared at the bottom of the orange sign that removing it might endanger others, this didn't stop some folks. This illustrates a characteristic that I have noticed in some tourists- an apparent increase in self-centeredness while on vacation.

An interesting side note happened in the summer of 1980. NBC news anchor Tom Brokaw showed up at Many Glacier. Two things I observed and particularly admired about him. First, he arrived with little fanfare and backpacked deep into the backcountry in a small party of four. They asked us for no special favors. They obviously wanted to truly experience the park with no messing around! Secondly, the only souvenir he seemed to want was one of the aforementioned orange signs. He didn't steal one from a trailhead, however. He was simply given a copy from our files. He did prove to be a little absent-minded, however, since he left behind a pair of boots which we mailed back to him.

On 28 August, I signed out and went off duty for the 1980 season and headed back to Illinois to again teach biology and coach track at Pittsfield High School. My first fully paid season at Glacier had been an eventful one, not just in terms of the previously mentioned occurrences, but also because of the day to day routine activities that made up the vast majority of our time and, in the process, beginning to make life-long friendships.

Campground Ranger Duties:
Upper Left – Manning ranger station information desk
Upper Right – Collecting fees at the campground kiosk
Bottom – Patrolling the Many Glacier Campground

Ranger Spangler entering information in the Many
Glacier station log.

Glacier - 1981

After a satisfying 1980 season, the backcountry position opened up at Many Glacier for the 1981 season. I was fortunate enough to be offered that position and quickly accepted. Being an outdoors person, this was a great opportunity for me. I love nature, had received survival training in the Army in Alaska, and a lot of cross training the previous two seasons that were pertinent to the backcountry position. I headed for Glacier with eager anticipation.

The following is the job description for the backcountry position as it was in Many Glacier at that time:

Responsibilities:
1. Monitor trail head signs
    A. Inspect bear warning signs (They are often stolen.)
    B. Current trail condition maps - Keep updated.
2. Trail patrols - as assigned
    A. Visitor contacts - day hikers & overnighters - Many times through contacts we can prevent problems before they arise.
    B. Trail conditions - Report status to supervisor. Note hazards and/or repairs needed.
    C. Campground - Demonstrate good camping techniques to visitors.
       - Visit with campers.
       - Prevent hazardous situations before they develop.
    D. Record trail conditions, etc. in the station log.
    E. Pit toilets - Set up a periodic cleaning schedule for each of them as well as keeping them supplied with toilet paper and lime, (one of the most exciting and romantic parts of the job!).

3. Boundary patrols
    A. Monitor domestic livestock trespass.
    B. Monitor area usage.
    C. Record & report vehicles seen at various boundary approaches to the park.
    D. Post and maintain boundary signs.
4. Do periodic maintenance and resupply of backcountry cabins.
5. Record/report wildlife sightings/counts, their activity, and where they occurred.
6. Keep updated on bear activity in our sub-district.
7. Maintain 4x4 vehicle in proper working condition.
    A. periodic inspection (air, oil, water, battery)
    B. Clean vehicle inside & out weekly.
    C. Keep storage box supplied with appropriate equipment.

Number 6 was the 800 pound gorilla in the room because a huge portion of my time dealt with bear activity. This was the case throughout the park but was (and still is) especially the case in the Many Glacier Sub-district which is a hotbed of grizzly activity in the park. Few people spend more time around free roaming grizzlies than Glacier backcountry rangers, and, again, that is especially true for Many Glacier backcountry rangers. I once asked bear researcher Kathy McArthur where she thought was the best place in the world to see them in the wild, and she replied - right there in Many Glacier. She was certainly an authority, having once appeared in a bear segment of 'Wild Kingdom' with Marlin Perkins.

Up until now, I have relied on my memory and the Many Glacier Station log for this narrative, but as a backcountry ranger, I also began keeping a personal patrol log. My primary responsibility now was to patrol the Many Glacier backcountry. In doing so, the ranger checks for such things as avalanche danger, bear or other wildlife hazards, and other unsafe trail conditions. This also involves EMS, search & rescue, and other visitor-related contacts. Monitoring visitor violations of park regulations are also important. Nothing could have been more different from school teaching, where your life involves always being at a certain place at a certain time. As a backcountry ranger, I was often on my own to decide my own patrol schedule. There was some paperwork involved, but a major portion of my time was spent in the backcountry, often alone. At those times, my connection with civilization was the portable radio on my hip (no cell phones in those days).

Any Many Glacier rangers could potentially become involved in life/death and lifesaving situations, but normally, as a campground ranger, I wasn't called upon to make significant life/safety decisions. As a backcountry ranger, I was often alone in the backcountry with the sole responsibility for deciding whether to close a trail or to open it, or whether cautionary signs needed to be posted for the safety of visitors. Is there fresh bear sign? Is there avalanche danger, or are there possible snow bridges to cross? These and other considerations are constantly on your mind. The feeling of responsibility is constantly there. Nevertheless, this was the dream job for me.

All Glacier employees receive orientation about bears. The park has more black bears than grizzlies but the focus is on the grizzlies. Backcountry and bear management rangers, however, receive more specialized bear management training. This 3-day program included firearms qualification for both the Smith & Wesson .44 magnum handgun and the Remington 870 shotgun. The handgun course was impossibly difficult. An attempt was made to recreate the adrenaline flow and emotional stress of a grizzly charge. Thus, we had to jog about ¼ mile before firing at a target 15 yards away. After squeezing off all 6 rounds, we had to run to a new location while reloading 4 more rounds. Then we were required to put 4 more well-aimed shots into the same target - and all 10 rounds within 25 seconds. Failure brought another one-lap run before trying again. Everyone except one person failed over and over again until all were exhausted. Finally, the standard was raised to 45 seconds, and the rest of us finally made it. The shotgun course was much easier, but did require a couple of shots from the hip (Bear charges often come suddenly and from close range, not giving time for a well-aimed shot from the shoulder.).

There was also training with tranquilizer kits as well as information on bear behavior. At that time, the bear drug that we used was called M-99. It has a long chemical name which I don't remember, if I ever knew it. What I do remember is that, if administered properly, it will put a bear down for about 4 hours while the necessary management activities are performed. That's the good news. The bad news is that even part of a drop through any membrane in the human body brings death in something less than a minute. Therefore, it was not to be handled alone. The antidote is called M-50-50. The partner of the contaminated person must very quickly administer this antidote to prevent death. The problem is that an overdose of this antidote can also kill the victim. Needless to say, I always feared these drugs more than the bears! M-99 was considered too dangerous by Canadians and today has also been eliminated by our Park Service.

Another problem with our tranquilizer system was the delivery process. We used a single-shot dart gun with drug-loaded darts propelled by a cap-like charge. Actually, there were 3 different charges, for 3 different distances. Therefore the cap had to be loaded in the field in the presence of the animal after estimating the range. As often as not, the critter then moved, forcing a re-estimate and reload. Your shot had to come within 50 yards or forget it! The dart needed to be loaded in the field also since the proper dosage was 2 cc for every 100 pounds of body weight, so the weight needed to be estimated, also. Pre-loaded darts were experimented with but proved to be wildly inaccurate. If everything went well and accurately with a good hit, the 'drop time' would be about 5 minutes. (The drop time is the time from initial injection until the animal goes down.) An angry bear can do a lot of damage in 5 minutes! The good news was that if everything went well, the M-99 would keep the animal down for a solid 4 hours (i.e. the 'down time').

We also trained in live-trapping. The procedure was different between front country situations and backcountry ones. In the front country, a culvert trap was (and still is) normally used. The culvert trap is just what the name implies- a section of metal road culvert closed at one end with a trap door at the other. This door is connected by wire to bait at the far end. The open door slams shut when the bear enters and pulls on the bait. It must be monitored constantly to assure that no curious visitors, especially children, go in and possibly trigger the door down on top of them, which could very well prove fatal. These traps are heavy and towed by vehicles, making them impractical for roadless areas. Where there are no roads the normal procedure was to set foot snares tied to the strongest tree one could find. This often involved V-shaped structures, home-made of logs containing the bait. We were soon to receive on-the-job training for the latter procedure!

On 26 June at about 1400 hours, two Many Glacier Hotel employees were on a day hike in the Feather Plume Falls area and were taking a lunch break when a young grizzly ambled toward them. These folks went up a tree while the bear ate their lunch. The animal remained in the vicinity about an hour and these young folks remained treed until it left. We got word of this that evening. All access trails into the area were then closed. On the morning of the 28th, Roger Shewmake, Regi Altop, and I headed out to Feather Plume to set a couple of the above-mentioned bear snares. We also had the assistance of a young man who was getting some on-the-job college-related experience. Nevertheless, with the four of us working, including the long hike in and out, this made for a very full day. We weren't able to head back until after 1900. We normally baited these traps with rotten beef or horse meat- the more odorous the better. We usually acquired this from road kills on the Blackfoot Reservation outside our eastern boundary. I had the honor of pushing this smelly package in on our wheeled litter. It actually made me somewhat nauseous. It proved to be an eventful day all around for Many Glacier personnel. While we were gone, an ambulance run was made to Cardston Memorial Hospital with a possible cardiac patient.

Once traps are set, snare warning signs must be posted in the area. These snares must be checked daily to assure that an animal isn't in the trap too long. This is to minimize possible injury to the bear and also to protect any wayward and curious visitor who might wander within the length of the snare cable. A grizzly caught in one of these goes absolutely crazy and a person within reach is in grave danger. Thus the next morning (the 29th) Terry Penttila, Dick Bahr, Dave Casteel, Shewmake, and Altop headed back to check the traps. Meanwhile I headed out on the Iceberg Trail with park bear researcher Kathy McArthur to check out a report of another grizzly in that area. When the trap crew checked the first trap, they found it had been torn apart - no bear. While proceeding to the second trap the young grizzly came out into a clearing to their front, paused and charged. Roger brought his shotgun to bear and Regi and Terry did the same with their handguns. They dropped the animal at just over 20 yards from them. It had 11 rounds in it.

This bear turned out to be a sub-adult sow. (A sub-adult is one that is recently weaned from its mama.) It wasn't too difficult to put together the scenario of why this young critter became so aggressive. These young animals are new at fending for themselves and older, larger adults have already staked their claim on most of the best forage areas. Therefore, these 'teenage' bears have probably already been chased away from prime feeding places. Thus, it is likely that this one was hungry and perhaps a bit desperate when it smelled these young folks' lunches. When it approached them, and they immediately went up the tree, the rest was easy. When she saw the rangers, she tried the same procedure again - only this time the people had guns and didn't run. This was a classic illustration of why people should not feed them - they tend to immediately begin to associate people with food, and the end result is: 'a fed bear often becomes a dead bear!' As a postscript to this story, the carcass was brought out on the wheeled litter that I had stashed the day before. It was autopsied to look for evidence of rabies or other abnormality that might account for its behavior and , as noted above, it was found to be simply a hungry bear, with too little body fat and, as a result, in poor physiological shape. Dave Casteel was along with his camera and documented the whole incident in sequence. I have since made a bear management slide program with this whole operation prominently included.

In addition to the ranger office, there were several other cabins in the employee housing area to which the emergency phone line was connected. Thus, emergency calls could be answered even when the office was closed. One of these lines ran into the cabin I shared with Regi Altop. We always intended to answer the phone before the second ring, and whoever got to the phone first took the call. On the evening of 30 June, I was the first one to the phone. This was the conversation as I recall it: Caller - "(heavy breathing) bear (more heavy breathing), big bear (more heavy breathing), ran all the way back!" Me: "Is everyone safe?" Caller:"Yes!" Me: "Then tell me your name." Caller - "unintelligible." Me - "Could you spell that for me?" Caller - "unintelligible." Me - "Could you give that to me more slowly." It is sometimes helpful and calming to ask and receive routine information, especially for that info that is needed anyway. In this case, the individual did calm down and told me his story. He and a fellow Many Glacier Hotel employee were fishing near the head of Grinnell Lake and had some fishing luck. At about 1915 hours on the above date, they turned around and saw a bear, apparently a grizzly, taking in the scene. They immediately went up a tree and remained there about 45 minutes. At some point, the animal disappeared up the slope toward the Grinnell Glacier area. The gentleman said that they had left all of their fishing gear at the lake and could we possibly go get it for them and, oh yes, one of them had lost a shoe during their retreat - could we possibly find and retrieve that also? I asked him to please go back with us tomorrow and show us where these items were. His answer was "I'm not going back there!". Regi and I went to the area the next day and found all the gear and the fish - all undisturbed! Yes, we even found the shoe near a tree which showed evidence of a very rapid ascent! All evidence indicated that the bear was simply curious, as bears often are. We had to wonder if the animal was as amused as we were at the image of these guys frantically heading up the tree and then racing several miles back to the hotel, one with only one shoe on!

Glacier is a special place, especially for biologists like myself, for many reasons. One of those is the fact that it is one of the few places in the lower 48 states that still has the entire complement of predators that was present at the time of the arrival of the European settlers. Because there aren't as many open areas as a place like Yellowstone, they aren't as often seen, but they are there. For instance, the park has as abundant a population of mountain lions as there is anywhere, but they are seldom seen. On 5 July, while Roger Shewmake and I were patrolling the eastern boundary, we caught what we thought was a brief glimpse of one crossing a meadow. In the several thousand miles that I have hiked in the park, that is the only one I have ever seen.

On that same evening, we got a call from a visitor that they had seen what appeared to be a climber falling on the slopes of Mt. Altyn nearby. Since the call came in late, a possible night rescue was in the offing. As we headed up the mountain, we were hit with rain and wind. Many of the plants in the harsh climate of Glacier have a protective waxy coating that become very slick when wet. This, as well as the blackness of the night, made it very difficult to even keep our feet, let alone find any climbers in trouble. At 2330, we received a radio call that the climbers had been found in the hotel bar. They were two ladies who had simply been fooling around on the slope, faking a fall. It was after midnight when we got back - cold, wet, tired, and not happy campers!

As a Christian, I have normally tried to avoid working on Sunday. Jesus picked grain on the Sabbath, however, for food for Him and his disciples, and this indicates to me that it is alright to do the necessary things then. We were involved in safety and service, so I have had no reservations about working on Sunday in most of my NPS jobs. In that vein, Sundays at Many Glacier were normally training days. On 19 July, for instance, Shewmake, Altop and I headed up to Grinnell Glacier for snow and ice rescue training. Glacier travel is dangerous and visitors are warned not to do it unaccompanied by a ranger. Even then ice axes, ropes, and crampons should be used. Some people don't heed the message, however, so we need to be prepared for a swift rescue. When anyone falls into a crevasse, life expectancy is normally less than 30 minutes because of hypothermia or suffocation if they happen to become wedged in. Since time is so short, a rescue cache is maintained right at the edge of the glacier so that, when notified, a rescue team can be air-lifted in with equipment already on-site. The sad truth, however, is that there was (and is) very little chance of anyone arriving in time.

In training on the glacier, we would practice on various skills such as glacier travel and various types of crevasse rescues. One of the basic activities was to rapell down into a crevasse and be 'rescued' by the others. On my first ever trip down to be rescued in 1979, I was initiated with tobacco juice on top of my head! We also did self-rescue in which, after rapelling down, we would ascend the ice wall on our own. I have actually found that descending and ascending an ice wall is easier than a rock wall because you can dig in with ice ax and crampons. Each one of these sessions was a full day. It is a 6.1 mile hike one way with a full pack and a 1600 foot elevation gain just to get to Grinnell Glacier. Thus, a very physical training session sandwiched between 12.2 miles of hiking meant we would sleep well that night!

At that time, the possession of firearms in this and other national parks was prohibited unless they were unloaded and broken down or cased. Due to a recent Supreme Court ruling, that is no longer the case. I strongly disagree with that decision, and one of the reasons is something that happened the very next Sunday. Shortly after 1700 hours on 26 July, we received a report of a possible gunshot wound in the upper parking lot of the Many Glacier Hotel. When we responded, we found the shooter and the victim in the hotel dispensary with the hotel nurse. It turned out to have been an accidental shooting that went like this: The gun owner was messing with his Ruger Super Black Hawk .44 Magnum handgun when it somehow accidently discharged. This is a powerful caliber and the round passed through a tool box, a car door, and then lodged in the back of another visitor. The bullet missed the spine by about an inch, and that near-miss plus the fact that the round was mostly spent when it hit the gentleman left him in surprisingly good condition. Nevertheless, we transported him to the hospital. I guess the gun owner expected to have to defend himself against a grizzly right in the parking lot! Another gun incident in which one of my cohorts told me of was of a city fellow found on a trail with his family intending to protect them from bears with a knife, a .32 caliber handgun, and a bow-and-arrow - none of which he really knew how to use - not that any of them would do anything but irritate the animal! I shudder to imagine coming around the bend in a trail and suddenly confronting a trigger-happy dude ready to unload on anything that moves!

There are a series of primitive one-room dwellings throughout Glacier called trail cabins. They are much like they might have been in pioneer times with a wood-burning stove, Coleman lantern, and an outdoor john. There are two of these in the Many Glacier sub-district - one close to the road (the Lee Creek cabin) and one in a more remote area near Slide Lake. They were equipped with outdoor toilets called 'low boys'. These are essentially a wooden box, open at one end with a modified opening on the other and simply placed over a large hole in the ground. These trail cabins are kept fully stocked with food and other basic essentials. They are way stations for NPS personnel using the backcountry and are not for public use. As a backcountry ranger, it was one of my jobs to see to their repair and resupply.

I planned to head in to Slide Lake on 28 July. The Blackfoot Indian Reservation borders Glacier on the east, and it is necessary to cross about 8 miles of it on foot to reach the Glacier boundary. From there it is another mile or so to the cabin. I was warned that a Blackfoot hunting party of about 30 horsemen was poaching in that area of the park, and the better part of valor was to postpone my trip. I had not yet done my firearms qualification so would be unarmed on the trip. I decided, however, to go anyway.

It was a cold and windy day and was spitting rain. The trail was muddy, and I began to pick up both fresh bear tracks as well as fresh pony tracks- lots of both! I also began to pick up the smell of rotten flesh. It wasn't until later that I found out that the University of Montana had set live bear traps baited with horse meat in the area, and it was obviously drawing them in. One set of tracks appeared to be a large boar in the 500 pound range. His tracks had a sharp edge (i.e. 'looking over your shoulder' fresh!). I began making plenty of noise so that there would be no surprises for 'anyone'. The rain, the thick brush, and the wind both muffled sound and limited visibility. The trip seemed to never end! The Slide Lake cabin was a welcome sight indeed! Since not all of the Blackfeet were friendly toward us, I left the windows boarded up so that it appeared unoccupied. Then I stoked up the stove, had a brief meal and prepared for bed. The Slide Lake area is a notorious 'dead' spot for radio transmission, and I knew that I was many miles from the nearest white man, so I went to sleep feeling very alone.

Early the next morning, I awoke to the sound of something large circling the cabin. I don't know to this day whether it was man or beast, but whatever it was, it eventually left. After finishing cleaning and inventorying the cabin, I headed out toward Gable Pass then down to the Belly River Valley and out to the trailhead near the Canadian border for my pickup ride. During the whole 2 day trip, I only saw one person - a trail crew worker in the pass.

On 1 August, we had another tiring training day of glacier training. This was particularly unfortunate for me because I was entered in the 12 mile Many Glacier Road Race the next day. I did manage to finish 5th in the race, which was better than my 9th place finish in '79. I don't remember if my time was better or not.

One route into Park Service employment can start in high school with the Youth Conservation Corps (YCC). Also, some colleges have a cooperative program with the government called the Student Conservation Association (SCA). In the YCC, students are often given some of the less pleasant jobs to perform and, of course, those requiring less skills. In the SCA, students may receive college credit, receive pay, or both, depending on the contract with the particular school. These folks often get to actually perform some ranger-like duties. As already mentioned, I went the VIP route. I bring all this up because in 1981 I had the added duty of being liaison to a YCC group. We fortunately had a good, hard-working group because they had the unenviable assignment of rehabilitating backcountry pit toilets. Mercifully, all I had to do was supervise and observe. The kids worked without complaint- at least not that I know of! They actually did better than me, as the following story will attest to.

On 11 August, I headed out to Poia Lake with the YCC crew for an overnighter. Late in the afternoon, we heard from a backpacker coming from Elisabeth Lake that a bear had been seen in one of the campgrounds there. Elisabeth Lake has been a hot bed for fishermen and therefore also a hot bed for bear activity since the anglers don't always dispose of fish entrails properly. I immediately radioed the ranger station so that the report could be investigated. Alas, my radio battery was almost dead and was kicking in and out of service. I could send a word or two on each surge of the dying battery. We were supposed to carry an extra battery for just such situations as this - but I had not done that. Therefore, the station received just enough to think that we might have a bear emergency in camp. Regi Altop, our bear management ranger, quickly rode the 6 miles by horseback to our aid. He had to spend the night with us under a space blanket sandwiched in the middle of a 12 mile round trip horse ride just because I hadn't followed protocol. This is one of those embarrassing events in the Park Service that I will always remember! I'm sure Regi won't forget it either!

All experienced outdoorsmen know the value of having a signal mirror with them to use in case of emergency - but what about at night? Fire guard Dick Bahr got the idea of carrying a strobe light like those used by downed military pilots. I picked up on the idea and purchased one also. I initially tried it out on the aborted night search that I previously mentioned. Those down below followed the location of our search team by my pulsing strobe and directed us to likely locations of the supposedly fallen climber. Although this had proven to be a hoax, our boss, Terry Penttila, remarked that he wished that we had a 'six-pack' of those. Thus, it was decided to check out the range of these strobes.

Swiftcurrent Mountain overlooks the entire Swiftcurrent Valley, including the ranger station. At the very top of that mountain is the Swiftcurrent fire lookout. On Monday, 24 August, I headed up to spend the night in the lookout building. The plan was to turn on the strobe up there at 2200 hours, and the folks at the ranger station would determine its visibility. Little did we know that this experiment was to become a real life situation!

In the early 1900's the Great Northern Railroad built a series of mountain chalets in what was to become Glacier National Park with the idea of attracting tourists to ride the rails to the area. Then they would ride horses to overnights at the various chalets. Only 2 of these chalets still exist, and one is on the west side of Swiftcurrent Pass just below the mountain and the lookout. Granite Park Chalet is located in an area so scenic that I can't even begin to describe it! This is still a popular place for back packers to have a roof over their heads overnight. It is a bit like going back in time since there is no electricity or indoor restroom facilities. Rooms are lighted by candles provided by the chalet staff. It is open only during the warm months and is so popular that overnight reservations must be made many months ahead of time. At the time of this story, they were still serving delicious homemade meals 3 times a day. (That is no longer the case since the cost became prohibitive, as all supplies have to be carried in weekly by horse or mule.) I decided to eat at the chalet that evening. It was a good time to do that since the staff had prepared a whole lot of 'Christmas' goodies. This 24th of August was their 'Christmas Eve.'(Yes, I said Christmas because there was a tradition among concessionaire workers to celebrate a summer Christmas with friends that they only saw in the summertime.) The fireguard manning the lookout had the same idea because he had come down to enjoy the festivities. When he and I headed up to the lookout, we had very full stomachs and were not moving very fast.

We didn't need to hurry, however, because the only deadline was the 2200 strobe experiment, and we still had plenty of time - or so we thought. It is only about a mile from the chalet to the lookout, but it is almost straight up, and I was carrying a full pack. It was beginning to sleet, and the wind was blowing so hard that our faces were being sandblasted with ice. Then my radio began picking up emergency transmissions from the Many Glacier Campground. Shortly after 2100, a 7-year old boy spilled scalding water on his arms, chest, and abdomen. The Alert 1 ambulance helicopter out of Kalispell, Montana, was quickly requested and was soon in route. The problem was that the chopper had to cross two mountain ranges with the winds high and the visibility poor. It was necessary that it go through Swiftcurrent Pass below us without hitting mountains on either side. We were called to put a light in the lookout so that the chopper pilot could use the building as a landmark to navigate the pass. The problem was that we were NOT in the lookout! It was definitely hustle time! We picked up the pace dramatically. At 2125, Alert 1 called that they were in the air with an ETA of 2150. They would reach the pass before that, however. With a full pack and a full stomach, I was beginning to feel nauseous, and we were running out of time. It seemed like forever when we finally reached the building. I turned quickly and saw the lights of the helicopter as it came down McDonald Valley, just to our west. While my companion frantically tried to unlock the door prior to locating and lighting the Coleman lantern, I thought of my strobe light. It would be quick, and time was running out. We hurriedly taped it high on a support cable and turned it on. We were about to find out its effectiveness for real! The strobe began flashing just before the copter reached the pass. We then heard the welcome words from the pilot that he had a visual on the light at the lookout. What a great relief it was to see the chopper lights as it safely negotiated the pass below us! I switched the strobe on again for the trip back to the hospital with the child. We often don't hear about the final outcomes of our medical efforts, and this can be a little frustrating. In this case, however, we were later informed that the lad was doing well. It was also gratifying when the parents thanked and complimented all the Park Service efforts on their son's behalf.

A last thing of note on the 1981 season is not really a noteworthy thing. One of the last entries in the station log on my last day of the season, 27 August, simply illustrates some of the strange characters we sometimes see in the National Parks. One of the other rangers actually made contact with the individual in question here and made the log entry shortly before I left. This guy camped illegally in Swiftcurrent Pass and claimed a unique "line of defense" against bears. He said that he strung fishing line around his campsite attached to an alarm clock which would go off when the bear tripped the line. He expected the alarm to scare the bear off. Good luck with that one!!

Anyway, I headed home with another good job performance rating on my record and anticipating the next season!

Bear Management Tools

Smith & Wesson Model 29 .44 magnum revolver

"Cap-Sur" dart gun, with darts

Remington Model 870 12 gauge shotgun
(with alternating buckshot & deer slugs)

A Glacier Grizzly. Note the muscled shoulder hump – typical of the species. (Photo by Ken Ward)

GLACIER - 1982

As I DROVE to Glacier in June of 1982, I was experiencing something new. For the first time I was going to be doing the same job in the same location in terms of my Park Service experience. Something else was new. I had finally completed my emergency medical technician certification back home that spring. This was important and invaluable for any ranger anywhere, but especially for backcountry rangers at Glacier since it was always possible that we might encounter a medical situation on the trail, a long way from any help except ourselves. It also did a lot for my hire ability rating.

I checked in at Many Glacier on 10 June. The day was not yet over before we responded to a fire alarm at the Many Glacier Hotel which, fortunately, turned out to be a false alarm. We no sooner got back from that when we got word of 2 grizzlies near the campground. Six of us responded in time to see the animals move harmlessly off in a northerly direction. This was a season when I definitely had to hit the ground running! The month of June, however, was, on the whole, a relatively quiet one. The main activities were training, answering false fire alarms, looking for missing hikers who all turned up safely, and generally getting our sub-district ready for the increased influx of visitors who would soon be coming in our short summer season.

Speaking of training, 30 June was memorable because of an unfortunate incident in which I was involved. A group of us were scheduled to go up to Grinnell Glacier that day to practice snow and ice travel while roping up with the use of ice axes and crampons. Part of this involved climbing the extensive and steep snow shoot to the Glacier Overlook. I was just in front of Dave Casteel when I slipped and began sliding toward an overhang and a long drop down. Before I could self-arrest, I hit Casteel and took his legs right out from under him. Although we were both able to arrest our fall before going over the edge, my crampons slashed his leg from knee to ankle. Dave gallantly took the blame immediately because we try to never be directly below the one just above us - and he was. The reason for that rule is because of the possibility of just such an incident. It was my fault too, though, for not digging my crampons in securely enough. Regardless of fault, it was a long walk back with an injured leg. Remembering the trail riding incident from 1979, I don't know why he would want to be around me anymore!

As before stated, Glacier is not a popular area for technical climbers. They prefer mountains with a lot of granite rock that is hard and holds climbing anchors well. The mountains of Glacier, on the other hand, are made up mostly of argilite which is actually just petrified mud and, therefore, relatively soft. Climbers don't trust it to hold a piton or any kind of anchor. They call this 'rotten' rock. Nevertheless, a reasonable number of people, either with or without climbing permits, do scramble up the heights. Therefore, we sometimes tried to pre-plan rescues in areas that are particularly popular and particularly hazardous. Some accidents also occur along popular trails and waterways. Ptarmigan Falls is one of those places. It is along one of our most popular hiking trails, and some people just get too close at the top. They don't realize how slick the wet, algae-covered rocks are. This occasionally results in someone going over the edge with serious or fatal results.

Thus on 17 July, Roger Shewmake, Regi Altop and I went up to create a pre-plan for Ptarmigan Falls. This is a lot better than trying to plan a rescue after the fact. Included in this planning was the location of two possible ambulance helicopter landing sites - time well spent.

On a less serious note, I ran across an entry I made in the station log on 19 July:

" 224B [me] has returned from Iceberg Lake - pit toilet cleaned & serviced; 'No Camping' sign replaced. The bugs were bad up there (i.e. I mean bug in the broader colloquial vernacular - not necessarily the true bugs, Hemiptera!) One actually bit me and drew blood. Does this constitute a 'bug mauling'?"

Speaking of maulings, and on a more serious note, our fish researchers had a history of bear incidents and maulings. We always recommend that people camping in the backcountry do not sleep in clothing with food smells on them. When these researchers have to handle fish all day long, it is almost impossible to get the fish smell off. Therefore, chief fish researcher Leo Marnell understandably began to request armed ranger escorts into the backcountry while on fish research projects. On 20 July, I was appointed to provide that escort for an overnight at Cracker Lake. This location has historically been a hotbed of grizzly activity. Even though bear diggings are sometimes found right in the campground, this particular project went off without a hitch. These folks do good work and constantly are trying to find ways to eradicate exotic (introduced) fish species from park waters while maintaining a healthy population of native ones. On this trip, they were specifically doing a survey to try and determine what fish were actually in this lake and also what was in there, historically speaking. As to me, other than guarding the folks, I did one of my favorite jobs, cleaning and servicing the campground pit toilet! One perk, however, was that I was able to scrounge some of the research department's food!

For me, as a backcountry ranger in Many Glacier Sub-district, most of my patrols were out-and-back day hikes with a return to the cabin at night. There were times where overnights in the backcountry were necessary, however, such as the previously mentioned supervision of the YCC kids. There was, of course, always the unexpected, and we always had our packs ready for an emergency. Therefore, we always had our packs with us, even at the office. In addition to things we needed for a more extended stay outdoors, we had emergency items for possible victims, also. Sometimes the overnights were totally routine, such as maintenance trips to the Slide Lake and Lee Creek trail cabins.

Speaking of overnights, on 26 July, I was dispatched to Poia Lake with park officials to re-locate the campground there. Care is taken in locating and designing backcountry campgrounds with camper safety as the primary concern. They need to be located in areas that are not flood or avalanche prone and are not along prominent bear travel routes. In this case, we re-located and re-designed this campground with these things in mind.

Occasionally, situations occur that are both serious and amusing, that is if everything turns out alright in the end. One such occurrence happened on 1 August. The Iceberg Trail was closed at that time because 3 different bears had been feeding along it. The normal procedure for monitoring a bear-caused trail closure was for one of us bear management people to patrol the closed trails. If we went 2 consecutive days without any fresh bear sign, or after a week's closure (which ever came first) we would open it up again. For the Iceberg Trail, however, we had an extra advantage. Across the valley from this trail is a high point which we came to call 'Bear Point'. From there, a good portion of the first part of that trail and the area around it could be observed. Not only could the area be scanned for the animals, but any persons who violated the closure could be observed without us being seen. On 1 August, I was at Bear Point glassing off the area, when I noted a single individual moving up the trail. All of a sudden, he stopped and froze in a semi-crouched position. Then the reason became clear. An adult grizzly was foraging only about 20-30 yards away.

They each then appeared to engage in a staring contest. I quickly radioed the station, and Altop and Shewmake headed up the trail to the rescue. As I guided them to the spot by radio, the interloper didn't move. I still wonder how a human being could stay in that awkward position for as long as he did (many minutes!). My two comrades escorted him out and, throughout it all, the bear didn't change position and showed nothing more than curiosity. He must have been thinking, "What is that idiot doing, anyway!" This hiker turned out to be a school teacher from Massachusetts and was lucky to get off with only a $25.00 fine! This didn't say much for my other profession! This particular teacher learned the lesson that when we closed a trail it was for a good reason.

The next day it was back to Bear Point - no 4-legged critters seen this time but 2 more of the two-legged variety. They also ended up 25 bucks apiece poorer. On the succeeding 2 days, it was the bear again. On the 4th, I had the longest continuous observation of a bear that I had ever made (almost 3 hours), but at least the humans were behaving themselves!

The day hike on 11 August was a very academic one. Fire guard Mark Glines and I escorted Dr. Bob Horodyski, an associate professor of geology from Tulane University, into the Appecunny Falls area. The area has some of the best examples of fossilized Stromatolite (a type of colonized blue -green algae) in the world. Items can be collected from the park only with a pre-approved collecting permit, and Dr. Horodyski had one. We helped him collect a 180 pound sample from the Altyn Limestone formation. Some scientists believe it to be about 13-14 million years old. We hefted it onto our wheeled litter (nearly acquiring a triple hernia in the process!) for a trip which eventually ended at the Smithsonian Institute in Washington, D.C. I hoped one day to view it there, but when my wife and I were visiting there many years later, I totally forgot to look for it!

We had a basic work schedule of five - 8 hour days on, and 2 off, each week. If we were in the area on an off day and an emergency occurred, we were morally obligated to respond, and it was rightfully expected of us. Nevertheless, it was (and is) important to get away from all that, so most of us planned to get out of the area on days off. You just need the break. Often it was something mundane like grocery shopping or becoming just another tourist and sightseeing elsewhere. Occasionally, however, some of us would do the same thing that we did on work days and hike, albeit out of our patrol areas. Some of us even formed a highly informal organization called 'The Glacier Marathon Hiking Society'. This consisted of rangers both inside and outside of our sub-district. We not only saw areas of the park that we wouldn't normally see, but as an added bonus, we learned more about it to pass along to visitors.

One such hike of our "society" was an overnight at Hole-in-the-Wall campground on 5-6 August. There were 5 of us on this trip to one of the most spectacular campgrounds in the park. It lies in a hanging valley and the setting is beyond description. Only a week later we were at it again. This time there were 11 of us on what was truly a 'marathon' hike. We left Logan Pass at around 0500 and headed out on the Highline Trail and had breakfast at Granite Park Chalet about 7 miles in. After that, we were almost constantly on the move with only a brief stop for a lunch out of our packs. This one day hike ended at about 1900 at Goat Haunt Ranger Station, a total of approximately 31 miles from our Logan Pass starting point. We picked up a boat ride to Waterton town site in Canada for a prearranged vehicle trip back to our respective stations. We were tired and sore but none the worse for wear after a trip along the Continental Divide through some of the most spectacular mountain scenery in the world. We talked about doing another marathon one-day hike - this one of 37 miles - but it never came about.

16 August, 1982 could have been my last. It started off routinely enough. Several of us along with some friends and family decided to climb up to the Iceberg Notch which towers above Iceberg Lake. This is a popular climbing route, and we wanted to get the lay of the land

for a possible future rescue. I debated whether to use my Alice pack with or without a frame. I was planning to break off from the group and spend the night at the Swiftcurrent Mountain Lookout. The frame would give me more support for additional baggage on this overnight. On the other hand, if the trip were to involve an actual hand-over-hand climb, a frameless pack would be preferred since it would wrap around my body better, thus keeping my center of gravity closer to the rock wall. Also the pack would be less likely to slide and affect my balance. Since we were planning to follow a mountain goat trail, and therefore involve only a steep hike, I opted for the frame. This was to prove very unwise.

We hadn't gone far on this goat trail before finding it extremely difficult to follow and finally losing it altogether. The scramble was on. It turned into a genuine single-file rock climb and I and my frame pack were not getting along well at all. Just ahead of me on the climb was Howard Snyder, a friend of Roger Shewmake and an experienced mountaineer. He had actually written a book about a tragic climb of Mt. McKinley (Denali) involving the death of companions. The name of it was 'In the Hall of the Mountain King'. Anyway, I digress. Howard became hung up above me, and I hung up also. Every time I looked up for a handhold, my head pushed the frame back and took my center of gravity away from the wall. I also was flying blind when I tried to look down to try to backtrack. I was stuck! A fall would likely carry me to the icy waters of Iceberg Lake far below- after perhaps bouncing off of a few rocks. My pack-laden body would likely go all the way to the bottom for a cold, watery grave. Suddenly, Shewmake slid behind me somehow and pulled the quick-release strap on my pack. Now able to see above and with Snyder now free also, I safely continued the climb to the top. Roger was even able to retrieve my pack. He did all of this while putting himself in great jeopardy himself. I will be forever grateful! After this, I separated from the group and spent a peaceful night on the top of Swiftcurrent Mountain.

The next incident of note occurred on the morning of 22 August on the Grinnell Lake Boat/Hike - the same one I used to lead in 1979. Park Naturalist Peter Watt had a group of 28 people along and was between Josephine and Grinnell Lakes when he saw a man running toward him and his group with a grizzly sow and yearling cub following close behind. Peter yelled for his folks to get off of the trail, and both the man and his group did just that. The bears kept going right on down the trail, snapping their jaws and growling as they passed no more than 2 or 3 feet from some people. There was no physical contact between bears and people, however. When we investigated the incident, it appeared that the animals just happened to be using the trail at the same time as the people with no particular aggressive intent. We couldn't take a chance though, and we closed the trail. By the way, this incident occurred at approximately the same location as the Millsap incident in 1979.

As mentioned before, when we had a bear-related closure it would be one of us bear management personnel that would patrol the trail and determine when it was appropriate to reopen.

Two consecutive patrols without any fresh sign of bear activity or one week, whichever came first, and the reopening would normally occur. I liked the procedure which I used in this case. Peter had encountered the bears at about 1100. The critters were moving east, and he and his group were traveling west. Thus, for two consecutive days, I hiked to the same spot at the same time and traveling in the same direction as the Watt group. However, the difference was I had a loaded Remington 870 shotgun in my hands and all the time looking for fresh sign. When no further sign of bears were found following the above protocol, the trail was reopened. Bears don't normally follow a pattern like that, but it's better to be on the safe side. Bear behavior patterns most commonly occur in regards to food gathering and foraging.

24 August was a 'circle the wagons' kind of day. This was a term that we used when everything seemed to happen at once. It was about 0730, as I recall, when it all started that day. I was in the middle of oatmeal and raisins when the emergency call came in. An 84 year old man had collapsed in the dining room of the Many Glacier Hotel while eating breakfast. He had been traveling with a tour group. Terry Penttila, Regi Altop, Dick Bahr, and I responded. When we got there, he was in full cardiac arrest. Kenn Rich and Norm Coy came shortly after. The hotel nurse and various other hotel personnel had already started CPR when we arrived. We then took over and rotated giving the CPR. (No AED was available at that time.) One would be giving mouth-to-mouth, another the chest compressions, a third timing the compressions, another holding the gentleman's false teeth, and a fifth on the radio. The poor guy had a history of heart problems, and we were only able to prolong the inevitable. Our protocol was that we were to continue CPR until we attained a heartbeat, we were too exhausted to continue, or a doctor or coroner declared the person legally dead. With neither of these individuals present, we continued for about 2 hours. This length of time was possible because of the multi-person rotation. A little known fact is that victims undergoing CPR often vomit, whether they recover or not. That was the case with this patient. Fortunately, I was not the one doing the rescue breathing when this happened! Sub-district Ranger Penttila had that unpleasant task at the time. Another thing that can happen, especially with elderly people like this one, is broken ribs. No matter how carefully the compressions are done, this happens, and such was the case with this gentleman. By the time my turn came to do compressions, his sternum felt like a piece of wood floating in liquid. It was actually difficult to keep it under my hands. We were able to contact a doctor by radio and, after relaying the lifeless vital signs to him, we heard a scratchy transmission coming back to us - "Cease CPR." We asked for a repeat - "Cease CPR." We had apparently been doing a good job with oxygen perfusion because when we concluded our efforts the body soon turned from a relatively normal color to slate gray. It is a memorable and sobering thing to watch a person's life drain away before your eyes.

In the middle of this episode, I was called away to check on a report of a grizzly in a nearby campground. I found none there. I got back in time to return to the rotation. Not long after this incident concluded we responded to a fire call. We ran to the fire cache and jumped into our turnout gear. It was a false alarm. 'Circle the wagons'. When I got back to my cabin the oatmeal was cold.

In reviewing the station log for this series of incidents, it is interesting to note the entries that follow. (See appendix #1) Entries became routine again very quickly. It is not that we had no feelings but this simply illustrated that life goes on, the emergencies and the routine, and we had to deal with both as the needs arose. It was, and is, important to be a professional. If one gets too emotionally involved in a situation, it will take its toll and may adversely affect the next task that needs to be done. I have never liked to work with those who were simply looking for thrills and adventure. I have a saying that the 3 most important things in the job are professionalism, professionalism, and professionalism.

This was a hectic end to my 1982 season since 25 August was my last duty day.

Heaven's Peak – as seen from Going-to-the-Sun Road

The marvelous 1982 Many Glacier Crew

Ranger Spangler 'on rapell'

Spangler doing a tyrolean traverse

GLACIER – 1983

AS THE '83 season approached, I had my first automatic rehire opportunity. If one was rated high enough from the previous season, the same position would be theirs the next year without competition. Such was now my situation. So, back I went to Many Glacier for another season as a backcountry ranger and checked in at 2000 hours on 15 June after more than a 2000 mile trip from Illinois.

June was a relatively quiet month again, as is often the case, since the visitor season is just getting started then. One thing that was going on was, in fact, an ongoing problem – garbage - particularly in the backcountry. In the front country (the developed areas that are available by car), garbage is picked up every day by contracted garbage haulers. Thus, it is not allowed to build up and attract critters, particularly bears. Also, the garbage cans are 'bear-proof' and have been very successful in that regard. The design for these mimic the design of your typical drive-up mail box. In the backcountry campsites, the situation was, and still is, more problematic. Campers are expected to pack their garbage out. Many apparently find this to be unpleasant. We often found garbage thrown down the pit toilets (outhouses) which provided a smorgas-bord for various animals. Marmots were digging under the toilets or simply going through an open door. Bears, on the other hand, could dig or simply tear the toilet down. The word came down from headquarters to get signs up posthaste in the campgrounds reminding people to NOT throw garbage down into them. Well, haste makes waste! Some homemade signs were quickly made up, and we scrambled in all directions to put them up. The sure place for them to be seen was to tack them to the inside of the toilet door. The unfortunate wording on the signs was: "Eat it or pack it out!" This crude misinterpretation quickly worked its way up to park headquarters, and just as quickly, we were given professionally prepared signs without any chance of misunderstanding. It was made clear that it was the GARBAGE that needed to be packed out! Needless to say, we got these signs up at least as fast as the previous ones!

Another embarrassing incident soon followed. This one, however, was on me personally. In fact, this was my most embarrassing moment in the Park Service, so far. It started with a dead deer fawn along the boardwalk at the upper end of Grinnell Creek. It had obviously been killed and partially consumed by a large predator - as to what kind, there were no tracks or other signs in evidence. It had to be assumed, however, that a bear had or would soon be on the carcass. I mentioned earlier the standard operating procedure for dealing with carcasses near trails. Although we preferred to close the trail and let nature take its course, this happens to be a main route to a boat dock frequented by concession tour boat patrons, and the concessionaire was losing money while the trail was closed. Therefore, it was quickly decided that this carcass would have to be removed. Thus, Regi Altop, Jeff Harvey, and I headed out at 1907 hours on 27 June to remove it. This involved canoeing across Swiftcurrent Lake, portaging ¼ mile to Josephine Lake, and then canoeing to the location involved. This was going to be a tense assignment no matter what, and it was getting close to dark. We began to joke around as we paddled, to release this tension. Earlier in the day we had firefighting training at the hotel, supervised by fireman Dick Bahr, and he had managed to ruffle our feathers during the exercise. Disparaging him as we paddled along dominated the conversation. Crude comments were also made in describing a deer relieving itself in the water. All of a sudden, we heard a siren and looked around to see our patrol car on the distant shore and heard a quick radio message:" Your radio is keyed!" All during the time we were making the undignified comments, Jeff had been inadvertently sitting on the radio in such a way that we had a live mike. When he turned to look at the flashing lights, he momentarily released the button allowing us to receive this transmission. Our conversation had not turned out to be the tension-releaser we had hoped for! I stated that I now needed to save a bullet for myself! We then fell back on the possibility that maybe Harvey's buttocks had muffled most of the more inflammatory comments. Later, we were to find out that, alas, this was not so. In fact, both Park Headquarters and the Many Glacier fire crew had recordings with amazing clarity. It was also obvious that the bulk of the conversation had been mine and that my voice carried well. Fire guard Kenn Rich made the understatement that we apparently had a morale problem. Roger Shewmake had frantically tried to override the transmission - but to no avail. What was worse - at the time of the incident Dick Bahr was presenting a class to concession employees with his radio on. There it was for all to hear! In fairness to Dick, he was a valued Many Glacier employee with many impressive skills, and this friction was only temporary. Nevertheless, it remains a part of Many Glacier lore.

Back to the deer carcass: With darkness approaching, we arrived and tied a weighted rope around its neck. As Altop and Harvey spread lime to kill the remaining smell, I stood by with my .44 magnum out and ready. My back was to the lake facing the thick vegetation nearby. This, plus the decreasing light, meant that I would probably hear any angry bear before I saw it. The deer was already in the canoe, but the liming process seemed to be taking forever (although, in actuality, it was probably only a few minutes). We pushed off with relief and gave the carcass the deep six out in the lake. This was one day that I was glad to see end!

Although we encountered no bears in the previous incident, Shewmake and I did jump one on the 28th. We were checking out the report of a grizzly near the trail in the Red Rock Lake area, and sure enough, as we rounded the bend of a trail in that area we found one grazing only about 25 yards ahead of us. It was not nearly as interested in us as we were in it and ignored us as we gave it a wide birth. Nevertheless, with a grizzly that close to a well-used trail, we called in an immediate trail closure.

At that time the Park Service had a system for supplementing the law enforcement division. This was called the Park Protection Commission (PPC). It worked like this: Selected non-commissioned rangers would take a one-week, 40-hour law enforcement instruction course. After that, they would be able to enforce and issue citations for minor misdemeanors such as parking or camping violations. Entrance station ranger Ernie Scherzer, campground ranger Bob Adams, fireguard Kenn Rich, Regi Altop, and I were picked to attend. The instruction began on 29 June. This program quickly fizzled out, however. I do not know specifically why it was discontinued, but I have a good idea based on the experiences I was later to have as a law enforcement ranger. Even minor violation contacts can occasionally escalate out of control without proper training and adequate defensive equipment. Regi and I would be armed for sure because of our bear management duties but would still be inadequately trained. Although a few rangers had been operating with that certification, I believe the government decided to no longer put inadequately trained personnel in harm's way. I agree. I do not believe that one can be 'sort of a cop.' It must be all or nothing.

As previously mentioned, the life of a ranger is not just one adventure after another. The typical day is often very routine. For example, on 1 July Shewmake and I patrolled the Iceberg Lake trail which was closed at the time due to bear activity. Although this patrol is never routine, cleaning the pit toilet at the lake was. We decided to combine our patrol with a little sanitary maintenance. As we were cleaning the outhouse, I couldn't help but comment that we were a bit over qualified for the job (Roger had a doctorate degree in nutrition, and I had a master of science in education). We both had a good laugh at our expense! By the way, we saw no fresh bear sign and reopened the trail.

Nevertheless, a report came in the next day at 1628 of a grizzly near the Iceberg trailhead. I headed out to observe. This looked to be a blond silvertip weighing about 200 pounds. When the animal moved to within 100 yards of the trail, I strapped on my shoulder holster and prepared to provide an armed escort out for the 9 people that were identified as being up there. When I had gathered all 9, we went past the grazing bear without incident, and I deposited these visitors in the Swiftcurrent parking lot at 1850. This was a "neutral" bear (i.e. It showed neither fear, nor aggression). Because it showed no aggression, we simply posted the trail with a 'bear frequenting' warning sign and left it open.

This incident illustrates a bone of contention that we backcountry/bear management rangers had with the park superintendent. He did not want us to have our firearms in view in routine situations (e.g. routine patrols). Our handguns were kept in our backpacks. As in the above case, they could be brought out in order to protect the public. The word came down that they were not for our personal protection. That was obvious since it was highly unlikely that we could ever reach our weapon in time to deal with a charging bear. When patrolling a closed trail, we would, of course, be locked and loaded. I experimented with trying to reach it quickly by utilizing the quick release strap on my Alice pack but was aware that this would not be nearly fast enough if the routine quickly became non-routine. I also began to wear pepper spray of the kind normally carried by postmen. (This was before spray was carried routinely.) Some of us thought that we might as well try it, since in the situation in which it would be used, we would have nothing to lose.

The next incident of note occurred on 9 July and had nothing to do with bears. At 1930 hours, we received a report of 2 missing Boy Scouts. They were part of a group that had climbed Chief Mountain. Bahr, Coy, Rich, and I hurried to the area, trying to beat the darkness. The lost boys showed up on the Chief Mountain road at approximately 2115. They had no rain gear, food, flashlight, or other survival gear. So much for their 'Be Prepared' motto! Chief Mountain stands alone and prominent in the northeast corner of the park and has a trail around the base. How they managed to get lost there is still an amazement to me! All they had to do was hike to the mountain from wherever they were. We got home after midnight. Oh well, overtime!

No rest for the weary! It was off to Slide Lake for an overnighter the next morning to check out reported vandalism at the cabin. The trail crew had been there first and had cleaned up after the vandals. Thus, the cabin was in surprisingly good shape. A couple of sleeping bags were missing though. It was nice to have the companionship of several other park personnel on this trip since this is a remote part of the park. After doing some work in the campground and inspecting the new 'low boy' john, we headed out via Gable Pass and the Belly River Valley. (By the way, low boys offer no privacy, except for the surrounding vegetation, but none usually is needed since these are used only in the more remote camping sites.) We had derisively nicknamed this low boy the "James Watt Memorial Privy" after the Director of the Department of the Interior at that time.

Going-to-the-Sun Road is the only road that completely transverses the park. It is also one of the most spectacular mountain roads in the world. The scenery from your car is absolutely breathtaking! The driver might not see it all, however, since his knuckles will be white on the steering wheel as the road is narrow and winding with many severe drop offs. There is supposedly a snow removal vehicle that is still at the bottom of one of these drop offs after going off of the road many years ago. Nearby is the mountain that gives the road its name - so called because the Indians believed that God traveled between the Earth and the Sun by way of this mountain. Shewmake, Penttila, Saint Mary Sub-district Ranger Jerry Ryder, and I weren't thinking about any of that as we rushed to the site of a fallen victim on the west side of Logan Pass. We had received the report of this at 1045 on 14 July and went immediately into rescue mode. At 1107 park- wide radio silence was declared which indicated we were becoming involved in a serious incident. Upon arrival we found Westside rangers already on the scene. We set up a rapell and Roger went over the edge while I acted as anchor man. Unfortunately, this turned out to be a recovery rather than a rescue - the poor guy didn't survive the fall.

We found out later, after an investigation, that this was no accident - but murder! The victim had been returning home after discharge from the military when he picked up a hitchhiker. He made the mistake of telling this hitchhiker that he had a fist full of discharge pay. The suspect had him stop at a pull off, supposedly to look at the scenery. After luring him to the edge of the cliff, he shoved him over. The man then stole both money and vehicle. He was later caught outside the park and prosecuted.

On 17 July I was involved in a less grim operation. A small black bear had been hanging out in the developed area and a decision was made to dart it and move it into a remote area. This area had been predetermined for any black bear that needed to be moved. Because black bear numbers were not in jeopardy, our patience with them was less than with the less abundant grizzly. Nevertheless, we tried to salvage 'garbage bears' when we could. Therefore, we would try to move this one for its own protection as well as for that of the visitors. If a bear starts associating humans with food, bad things happen, and someone was bound to feed it eventually if it were to continue hanging around.

This particular operation went very smoothly, which was a good thing, considering that we didn't get started until late afternoon. We cruised the road with Regi and I in the back of the pickup. The bear showed up just a couple of minutes after we started, conveniently along the road as we came around a bend called 'sheep curve'. Regi was able to dart him right from the back of the truck. It took about 5 ½ minutes for him to go down. He turned out to be a 123 pound she. I stood by with my .44 at high port while the numbered ear tag was placed. Her personal history would later be put on computer with that number in our Bear Information Management System (BIMS). If she showed up again, she could be easily identified as a previous transgressor and would probably have to be put down. After the processing was done, she was administered the M 50-50 antidote and loaded in our mobile culvert trap for Altop and me to take to the release site. We got back at 2215 with an efficiently earned 5 ½ hours of overtime.

A brief change of pace occurred on the 18th when I got a radio call from Penttila. He asked if I wanted to see the models. I answered in the affirmative - It's always good to answer in the affirmative with the boss. I wondered if he was talking about automobiles, boats, planes ...or what. The only other thing he said was to meet him at the hotel. When I got there, the question was quickly answered. They were models doing an advertising shoot for Early Winters catalog. We met them and exchanged pleasantries for a while. This was a nice change of pace from our regular duties! I don't believe that the company is still in business, but I used to order outdoor/camping items from them occasionally. I still have the catalog with the pictures from that Many Glacier shoot.

There is nothing like a Glacier hailstorm! One time while I was working at Many Glacier, it sounded like a locomotive was headed down Swiftcurrent Valley, and it turned out to be the most spectacular one I ever saw, and we were pelted with golf ball-sized hail stones for a prolonged period of time until they totally obscured the ground. Fortunately, it occurred late in the day when most of us were in our quarters. We heard that some late returning hikers got some pretty good bruises, however. Regi and I weren't so lucky on the 23rd. While on a routine canoe patrol to check fishing permits and life vests, we were hit by a sudden sharp hail storm which caught us in the middle of Stump Lake. We hugged the south shoreline and made it to Birch's boat house for shelter. I'm glad that the folks there took us in because those hail stones really stung! Storms can come on quickly in the mountains, and I have been hit by hail, rain, sleet and snow before - all in the same day!

A decision had been made higher up to expand our grizzly bear research program to include, for the first time, the radio-collaring of bears-of-opportunity. This procedure had already been done on the Blackfoot Reservation east of the park by University of Montana researchers, but had not yet been done in the park. Our sub-district, among others, was given the equipment to do so whenever the opportunity presented itself. This was thought to be another good way to learn about these fascinating creatures that would supplement direct observation and the collection of bear droppings (I've studied plenty of droppings but, fortunately, have never had to actually collect any!). This collaring opportunity was soon to present itself to us at Many Glacier.

A sub-adult blond grizzly had been hanging around for a while. It was not aggressive but also showed no fear of people whatsoever. I watched it waltz right through a group of tourists one time. It was almost certain to eventually get human food or otherwise get into trouble with this kind of behavior. Thus, it needed to be moved anyway and was a good candidate for the collar.

As mentioned earlier, one of many things that I liked about the backcountry position was the lack of structure. This is just the opposite of school teaching which made it a nice summer change. Although I was assigned various tasks, on many days I set my own agenda. If it was a routine day, I tried to rotate patrols on our various trails. 28 July started out as one of those kind of days. I had planned to patrol the Iceberg Lake Trail that day. To this day I don't know why, but I woke up that morning with a very uneasy feeling about doing that. I always had a bit of healthy, alert-causing fear in the pit of my stomach when hiking Glacier trails, particularly when alone, which was much of the time, and no more on this particular trail than any other. That morning, somehow, it was different. It is not particularly flattering to myself to confess that this was the reason that I suggested to Shewmake that we go for the young grizzly that day. It made sense anyway because it was bound to get into trouble sooner or later, and Roger and I would be headed home within the month, leaving only Penttila and Altop as bear managers at Many Glacier. Everyone agreed and thus the dye was cast. Roger, Regi, and I would go after the bear which had become known as "chocolate-legs". An unsuccessful attempt had actually been made on the 20th in which I did not take part. Shewmake, Altop and Bahr, suffered through a missed shot, an erratic dart flight, and a gun jam on the 3rd attempt before the whole operation was aborted. As I have mentioned previously, this is an imperfect system.

On this second attempt, everything went smoothly at first. We quickly located the animal that we were looking for on the slopes of Mt. Altyn. It crossed the road at Sheep Curve, bolted right through a group of visitors, and ended up on the slope below the hotel water site. We found it in a day bed at the base of a small cliff. This seemed perfect. We positioned ourselves just above the bear at the top of this cliff/rock outcrop in a secure position with a close and clear shot to be had. Regi darted it in the hip with what would seem to have been a solid hit. Then everything went south! The dart apparently rebounded off of the pelvic bone with a twang. The critter ran into thick brush, and we had no idea how much of the M-99 was in the bear and how much was still in the dart - and we did not know where either was! Altop, Shewmake, and I started after it through brush so thick you could barely see your hand in front of your face with a bear out there somewhere that just might be taking offense at being shot at. I climbed up on a large boulder to get a better look. I had my handgun at the ready, and Roger and Regi continued to trudge ahead, Shewmake with the shotgun and Altop with the dart gun. Things were getting tense. I could hopefully see brush move before the charging animal could reach my friends or myself. We tried to make sure that we stayed in close radio contact so that I didn't mistake the movement of the other rangers for the bear. They didn't see the animal until they were only a few feet away. Fortunately, it had received enough of the drug to put it down, but not out. A supplemental dosage was administered with the dart pistol - first crisis over.

The fireguards assisted us with the ear tagging and the radio-collaring and the collection of research data. While others did that, I provided cover with my handgun. The difference in danger between black bears and grizzlies was illustrated here. With the black bear, I had merely stood by with my weapon at high port. With the grizzly, I had the gun pressed against the back of its neck the whole time we were working on her. (Yes, it turned out to be a 116 pound sub-adult female.) After this processing was done, she was taken by helicopter in a sling load to a pre-determined release site in a remote area near Pinchot Creek. Regi and Roger went with the pilot (Krueger) and administered the antidote, waiting only long enough to make sure that she was fully recovered.

Meanwhile, back at the ranch, Dick Bahr, Brian Adams, and I had the unenviable task of finding the errant dart. We knew that it was out there somewhere in the thick brush. We also knew that it was still partially filled since only part of it ended up in the bear. This operation occurred close to the road and the hotel, so we had to assume that visitors might end up exposed to it. Nevertheless, the first people that might be exposed to it was us. As we looked, it was in the back of my mind that one of us might step on it with disastrous results. Fortunately, Dick found it hanging on a branch just waiting for someone to run into. Crisis ended. Anyway, the first radio-collaring of the first grizzly bear in Glacier National Park history occurred on 28 July 1983 at Many Glacier because I did not want to go to Iceberg Lake!

A postscript on this story: The radio collar had to be put on carefully to be big enough to allow for growth and small enough not to come off. The radio battery was designed to last 3 years and the collar was designed to rot off in 3 years. This is precisely what happened. The collar was found 3 years later after providing 3 years of valuable data and the bear, as far as I know, didn't cause any more trouble. I still have part of the original collar as a souvenir.

The next day several of us went to St. Mary for rescue training, and it turned out to be another tense experience because the training leaders over there did not use the same safety protocols that we were used to. This made for a long day - At one point, I declined to repel over the edge because I felt that their procedures were not safe enough.

30 July proved to be a sad day for the Glacier family. A son of Jerry Ryder, St. Mary Subdistrict Ranger, was tragically killed in a 4-wheeler accident that evening. East side emergency people responded quickly to the site just east of the park as well as the Alert ambulance helicopter from Kalispell, but to no avail. The funeral was on 7 August, and it was a period of time we would all like to forget.

I absolutely HATE to fly! ('Scared' would probably be more descriptive.) I avoid flying like the plague. Sometimes I have found it unavoidable, however. In my army days, Uncle Sam was not sympathetic to alternate travel arrangements. Thus, plane travel was often unavoidable. Such was also the case on the evening of 5 August with the NPS. A young man had run all the way back from Red Gap Pass, exhausted and distraught. He stated that his brother had collapsed and needed help. It had been a warm day, especially by Glacier standards, and from the description of the situation, we suspected possible heat exhaustion or heat stroke - a true emergency. The best option at the time was to call for Krueger's private helicopter. He had a contract with the government for just such emergencies. This chopper would only seat 3 people which turned out to be Shewmake and me, in addition to the pilot. He picked us up at our helipad at Many Glacier. Roger had soaked a bed sheet with water in anticipating the problem. The victim's brother had left him in a semi-conscious condition with others of the party at about 1400 hours, so we didn't know what we were going to find.

This chopper was one of those that has a bubble canopy and is open on the sides. I had the dubious distinction of sitting on the outside. This is the type of situation that causes me to check my seat harness about 5 times! We lifted off at 1813 hours. As we approached the Ptarmigan Wall, groaning with a full load of people and medical equipment, the ground began to rise rapidly to meet us. A mountain goat running just below us seemed almost close enough to touch. At about this time, Krueger remarked casually," I don't know if we are going to clear this ridge or not." What!! We did clear it though - barely! All of a sudden, the ground dropped off of the table on the other side and was thousands of feet down. By this time, I may have been in worse shape than the victim! We touched down at 1824 a little ways above the victim, only 11 minutes after we had lifted off, but it seemed a lot longer to me!

We found him with his wife and his brother's wife. It was good that he was only 22 years old with an uncomplicated medical history. He was conscious with relatively stable vital signs but was nauseous. He was able to walk to the chopper with assistance. Roger was good enough to let me fly out with the patient while he took the long hike out in the middle of the night with the 2 ladies. Although we got back at 1922, and Shewmake and his group not until 2330, I would have preferred to stick to terra firma. I joked with Roger later, telling him not to do me any more such favors! The next day Dick Bahr and I hiked in to Red Gap Pass to retrieve the visitors' packs. It was about 10 miles round trip, as I recall, but we were used to that, and at least it was all on terra firma! An interesting side note to this story is that trail crew leader Dave Shea reported a sow and 3 cubs in the same area that same morning. Roger said that he was glad he didn't know that the night before! We saw no sign of them, by the way. As a postscript to this story, district ranger Dallas Koehn called to apologize to Shewmake for the night time walk out which he did not intend to happen. Krueger apparently didn't get the word about a double trip.

Important visitors showed up in the park in August. Vice President George H. W. Bush and his entourage came for a visit and it stirred up some excitement, but not so much for us since he didn't come to our area. Then Senator Pat Williams and Park Service Director Lorraine Mitzmeyer came and were in the valley for a while, supposedly on their way to a seminar/symposium at Waterton in Canada. This was on the 11th, but Regi Altop and I were otherwise occupied then. On the 15th, a group of foreign diplomats came after reserving no less than 20 campsites in the Many Glacier Campground. Anyway, back to the 11th.

A little after 1330, we received a report of a bicycle accident on the Chief Mountain Road near the Canadian border that appeared to involve serious injuries. Regi and I were immediately dispatched in our ambulance and arrived in about 30 minutes. The victim turned out to be a young lady who was a member of a bicycle touring group from Pittsburg. She was a medical professional (physical therapist), and that perhaps at least partly accounted for her calm demeanor in the face of fairly significant trauma. She had skidded in some gravel on the shoulder of the road and was thrown over the front of her cycle. She landed on her head. Her glasses were broken and was bleeding from the face and had various lacerations and bruises on her body. The most ominous symptom, however, was some numbness in her upper extremities. Because of this and the mechanism of injury, we had to consider the possibility of spinal injuries.

We had a legal complication to treatment, however. There was a doctor in the group who was a specialist at a Pittsburg hospital. Technically, he was legally considered to be the most qualified to treat the patient - but he had little or no experience in dealing with medical emergencies in the field. He was more than willing to stand back and let us deal with this. To cover ourselves legally, we began to ask him appropriate leading questions such as, "Doctor, don't you think that we should check for glass in her eyes?" or asked him if he didn't think we should provide spinal stabilization. Fortunately, he followed our leads, and we worked our way through the correct procedures. After packaging her up, we loaded her for transport to Cardston, Alberta Hospital. This was our 'go to' hospital for most situations. Regi drove, and we asked the doctor to take a cycle of vital signs to relay to the hospital. He hesitated and then answered that he always had a nurse do that. Thus, I stayed in the back and took them. This was an eye-opening experience for me in realizing that every doctor is not necessarily prepared for emergency medical situations.

It turned out that the lady had a broken right clavicle in addition to the cuts and bruises and was expected to fully recover. We had no sooner finished at the hospital than we were called to back up the St. Mary ambulance for a medical emergency at Rising Sun Campground. The report was of a young lady jogger with cardiac-like signs and symptoms. St. Mary ended up handling the situation without requiring our support, so we aborted the run and were back home by 2130.

On 13 August, Dick Bahr, Scott Schuster (teenage son of naturalist Bob Schuster), and me hiked into Cracker Lake. We had 4 purposes in this patrol. 1. To measure the trail (with measuring wheel).; 2. Photograph and diagram the campground. 3. Clean the pit toilet; and 4. Check out a goat carcass in the area of the campground. I was the only one armed, so the other two started the campground housekeeping while I headed out beyond the edge of the campground to check out the carcass report. This took me into a large thick patch of alder bushes that were about chest high - high enough to hide a carcass or a bear who might be guarding it. Nevertheless, tense situations like this were part of what I was being paid for. I neither saw nor smelled a carcass nor any bear, so I went back to help finish the other tasks, and opened up the previously closed campground. This has been a recurring situation at that campground - closing it because of bear activity and then reopening it again when that activity ceases. I have felt that this campground should be permanently closed because of the frequency of the bear activity there. In fact, I felt so strongly about this at the time that I put it in writing. Anyway, we did see fresh diggings in the campground, and a black bear on the way back as well as taking a grizzly report from a concession wrangler. Therefore, a 'bear frequenting' sign was posted on this trail.

One of my last official acts of the summer was to help work on the new ranger fitness trail. To this day, I don't know if it was ever finished and used, but the idea was good. The most noteworthy thing about this for me was a log entry that I made at the end of the day after working on the project on the 20th: "224B, 524A back from Chlorinator Road: no hucks, no runs (scat), no bears!" I guess once a baseball player- always a baseball player!

The annual Many Glacier Road Race was held on the 21st, but mercifully, I was elsewhere and didn't run in it. Dick Bahr and I headed out to the Lee Creek Cabin to inventory, clean and do some maintenance. Lee Creek and Slide Lake are the 2 patrol cabins in the Many Glacier Sub-district. As mentioned before, Slide Lake is in a remote area, but the Lee Creek one is no more than a half-hour hike from the Chief Mountain Road. Both, however, are straight out of the 1800's.

Near the end of the season brought the annual "Nattie Awards". The interpreters gave out awards to each employee reflecting our idiosyncrasies. I had commented that they had nothing on me. Boy was I wrong! 'Nuf said! This was a fun evening for everyone and was just one more indication of the family atmosphere that we had there. Although these awards were all in fun, I received one serious one at the end of the season - a certification of completion for basic rescue techniques. This was one more thing to add to my resume.

My last duty day of the season was 22 August. That last day was mostly administrative, as the last ones usually are. After another good evaluation, I signed out, packed up and headed back toward Illinois. At that time, I did not know that this was to be my last season at Many Glacier.

Bear Management Activities

Spangler closes trail because of grizzly activity.

Spangler covers while Dick Bahr applies the first radio collar to the first grizzly in Glacier Natl. Park history.

Spangler and SCA student working on the construction of a backcountry live trap.

Backcountry Ranger

Spangler, pointing to a stromatolite fossil, one sample of which he and Mark Glines were helping To collect for the Smithsonian Institute.

Ranger in the Glacier backcountry

Resting in the backcountry

1984

AFTER ACHIEVING A performance rating that gave me automatic rehire for the Many Glacier backcountry position once again, I assumed that I would be doing that in '84. There was a catch, however. Both Penttila and Shewmake had left and there were new supervisory personnel there. Not only was there no residual loyalty for me, but 2 of the 4 bear management people (Shewmake and Penttila) would not be there. The new supervisor was not willing to have a 3rd bear ranger (me) there for only 3 months - He wanted 6 and wasn't willing to compromise. This was, of course, a no go with my teaching schedule. Therefore, I had to very regretfully decline the position. It was too late to go anywhere else, so I was not going to work for the NPS for the first time in 5 years. I was bitterly disappointed, but I could understand the situation somewhat. A new supervisor, not as familiar with the job, is much more reluctant to be left shorthanded during the season, especially with emergency response-related positions.

Thus, I spent the summer on the other side of this subject - as a visitor to various parks and making slide programs of them. I did manage to find time to lead a group of men from my home area on a canoe trip into the Boundary Waters Area in Minnesota (my 8th trip up there). This is a marvelous resource, and one of the most extensive unspoiled areas left in the lower 48 states. It also helped me to keep my outdoor skills sharp.

This makes for a very short chapter to this book!

ISLE ROYALE NATIONAL PARK -1985

MY SEPARATION FROM the Park Service was only a one year hiatus. In the summer of 1985 I accepted an interpretation position at Isle Royale National Park in Michigan. This is actually an island in Lake Superior that is about 45 miles long and 9 miles wide at its widest point. Except for 2 small developments at either end of the island, it is totally undeveloped wilderness. It is known as a backpacker's paradise and the home of a prolonged predator/prey relationship study in regard to the wolves and moose that are there.

I had been there before as a church counselor on a backpack trip for a group of teenagers and found it a great experience. Thus, I looked forward to the season even though my job was to be manning the visitor center on the mainland in Houghton, Michigan. I did get to spend about 2 weeks on the island during orientation. The park is so remote that the only way out there is by a multi-hour boat trip or by float plane and there are no roads, only foot trails - like I said, an outdoorsman's paradise! I did get some extensive hiking in while I was out there and noticed a different feeling that, at first, I couldn't explain. The terrain was certainly different from Glacier but that wasn't it. Then I realized that the difference was bears. Isle Royale has none. I didn't have that healthy low-grade fear in the pit of my stomach that increased my alertness. I wasn't constantly checking the wind, blind turns in the trail, and bear-friendly vegetation. No need to look for fresh bear sign either. Wolves are the only large predators on the island, and they avoid people like the plague. Anyway, when orientation was over it was back to the mainland.

This job was day and night different from what I had known at Glacier. Instead of out on the trail, it was into the office. I was simply helping to run the visitor center. I did end up presenting one slide program. This was also my first experience with computers. All of the staff spent time using our computerized reservation system to schedule boat trips to the island. The Ranger III, our NPS boat, would go out one day and come back the next. I didn't get along well with computers then and I still don't. There were some good things about the job, however. For one thing, I made out like a bandit, monetarily. The Chief Ranger and his wife were to be on the island all summer and needed someone to look after their mainland home. I was able to live in their house for only $25.00 a month. The only stipulation was that I had to look after their garden, send veggies out to the island, and to ride herd on their teenage son. Overall it was a good deal. My parents also were able to visit me for the first time as a park ranger.

Other job firsts for me were operating a cash register to sell park-related items and directing traffic for people coming to get on the boat. I also aided in mooring and unmooring the boat. All of these activities were pretty mundane compared to what I had known but did help to add to my resume. Although I was already an experienced canoeist, I received some valuable motorboat training in Lake Superior. I had been on motorboat patrols at Glacier but mostly with someone else piloting the vessel- thus, this was also valuable training. I had received my Type I firefighting certification at Glacier and was able to renew it here. The rest of the job, of course, involved greeting visitors and answering their questions. My final evaluation was a good one, but both my supervisor and I realized that I would rather be outdoors. Thus, was my 1985 summer.

I need to add one footnote at the end of this chapter. One other thing was different this year, and from now on, in this book. At Many Glacier, I had access to the station log and relied on it heavily in writing those chapters. I also used my personal patrol logs plus, of course, my memory. From here on out, I have to rely just on the last 2 sources plus my personal field notes. In no other place that I have been has there been a station log - at least none that I was ever aware of. I have always found that unfortunate because it was a great way to keep everyone aware of what was going on, and knowing where everyone was all the time. You signed out where you were going and signed in when you got back. This was important, personal safety wise. It also facilitated the team feeling in accomplishing the overall mission.

Aerial view of Isle Royale National Park

One of the few ways to get to Isle Royale: the NPS boat, the Ranger III.

A key predator- prey relationship:

wolves & moose

Key Isle Royale wildlife

Beaver

Photo by
Rolf Peterson

Timber wolf

Photo by
Scot Stewart

Moose

Photo by
Rolf Peterson

GLACIER NATIONAL PARK - 1986

ALTHOUGH I QUALIFIED for automatic rehire, I didn't want to be cooped up indoors again at Isle Royale. Nevertheless, my availability still wasn't long enough for the Glacier season. Then out of the clear blue, I got a call from Roger Shewmake. He was coming out of his brief NPS retirement and had hired on as a backcountry ranger in the Two Medicine Sub-district in the southeastern part of Glacier. He asked if I would join him there. He said that he needed another experienced backcountry/bear management ranger to back him up and that he was the only one there. The only way I could do that with my short season was to come as a Volunteer in Park (VIP). Not only was I glad to get back to Glacier, but I could hardly refuse a good friend who had also saved my life! Thus, after a 2 year absence, I was headed back from whence I had started.

At Many Glacier, I had lived in a 2-person cabin with an assigned fellow employee, the last 4 seasons with Regi Altop. The cabin was rustic and small, but comfortable. Regi was easy to live with. As a Morman, he neither smoked nor drank, so I didn't have to deal with any of that. He was easy-going and easy to live with, and I don't ever remember profanity coming out of his mouth - an all-around good man and a good ranger. At Isle Royale, as already mentioned, I had the run of a nice ranch house. Two Medicine was much different, however. They had no housing for me at all. Thus, when I got out there I purchased a used Apache trailer, parked it outside the Shewmake residence and plugged in to their electrical outlet. There was only room in there to eat, sleep, and sit but I spent most of my down time over at the Shewmakes' anyway.

My "official" job title was backcountry VIP. My duties were essentially the same as at Many Glacier except that I would get only subsistence pay. The job title illustrated an interesting situation. Backcountry rangers were always armed, and I was to do the duties of a backcountry ranger. VIPs, however, were not armed - an interesting conflict of interest. I solved it by simply carrying my .44 magnum concealed in my pack (That's what we all did anyway.). It was helpful that I owned my own gun. Then I simply used a "don't ask, don't tell" policy. Roger was the only one that I openly discussed this with. Nevertheless, the supervisory personnel had to know that I was 'carrying' because my ammo pouch was in plain view on my belt. I believe that it was simply a matter of them choosing not to know - then they didn't have to deal with the dilemma.

My first backcountry patrol was on 20 June, and it proved to be a routine 10 miler. My mood was reflected in an entry that I made in my personal patrol log: "It's nice to be back in the saddle again!". Another routine patrol occurred the next day but with an added twist. Regi Altop had come over and accompanied me on the hike - just like old times! Although it was good to have Regi along, it was a cold and windy trip.

The next day began routinely enough. Then in the PM visitors told me that a black bear was sitting on the Mt. Henry trail - about a 100 yards up. By the time I got there, it was gone. While returning from this, I received an emergency call to go up the South Shore Trail past Paradise Point for a medical situation. When I got there, I found a 68 year old man lying against a log shouting "Jesus, Jesus, please help me Jesus!". His wife was standing helplessly over him. Shewmake had responded also. We found out that he had a heart condition and was suffering severe angina pains. To make it worse, he had left his nitroglycerin medication back in his car, and we were several miles from the road. This was obviously a time for a helicopter evacuation, but everything seemed to be going wrong that could go wrong. First, the Alert I chopper out of Kalispell was on another run. That left us once again with our backup - Krueger's sightseeing bird, which didn't have advanced medical supplies on board, nor a stretcher. To make matters worse, the area was thickly wooded with nary a single suitable landing site around.

Therefore, we called for a stretcher, the nearest being about 20 miles away, and I stayed with the victim while Roger went to look for the nearest suitable clearing. I was hoping that the gentleman did not go into cardiac arrest while Shewmake was gone, because one-person CPR can only be performed for a limited time, even when the performer is in excellent physical condition. We not only needed a stretcher, but a couple of extra bodies as additional stretcher bearers. We called for recruits by radio. After what seemed like an eternity, the stretcher arrived with a garbage man who was collecting in the area at the time, along with the son of a park employee who also happened to be available.

In the meantime, Roger had found a landing site and reported that it was about ½ mile away through the woods and brush. After loading up the victim, the 4 of us struggled our way through the woods while hauling the stretcher. Fortunately, we didn't have to wait long as Krueger had followed Shewmake's map coordinates accurately, and he was guided in for a successful landing. The feeling of relief was palpable as we watched the takeoff with a live subject!

One of the frustrating things about our EMS responses in the NPS is that we often don't get to find out the end results of our efforts. It is always good to know how things turn out for a patient. In this case, however, we did find out. His circulatory problems proved severe enough that amputating his left foot was considered. In the end, though, the foot was saved - a gratifying end to a very difficult situation! As I recall, we got a letter from those folks thanking us for saving his life - making everything even more gratifying! Nevertheless, we didn't ever want to face such an unfortunate set of circumstances again, and tried to think of ways to fix things - more on that to come.

The next medical emergency occurred on 28 June and turned out to be a relatively minor one. A 14 year old boy had dropped the corner of a U-Haul trailer on his leg in the Two Medicine Campground. Our transport was not needed as his parents took him to Cutbank Hospital to receive a total of 18 stitches to close his upper thigh wound.

The rest of June into the middle of July was marked by seemingly constant wind, rain, cold, and, yes, even snow! As I said above, we didn't want to go through another helicopter lift out without known landing spots in the area. Thus, we had already begun the process of mapping out satisfactory sites in the sub-district as we did our routine foot patrols. As important as this was, I was getting mighty tired of being cold and wet all day, and most every day. Cleaning and servicing pit toilets during this time didn't make it any more pleasant either! An entry that I made in my patrol log on 11 July read: "Will we never see the end of rain, wind, and snow?" A canoe patrol and a motor boat patrol during this time period were nice changes of pace along with occasional good weather and sunshine.

At Many Glacier, we had an ideal area to practice mountain rescue training. It was called Wilbur Cliffs. It was only a short hike from the station and included several cliffs in a U-shaped formation and only about 50 or so feet high. This made it possible to get multiple repetitions in without time-consuming descents and ascents, since the main skill factors involved are in the beginning of these activities. Having more than one wall and a chasm in between made possible more than one activity going on at a time. Although the short distance to the area meant that not much work time was consumed going to and from, it was just secluded enough that we were not interrupted by visitors. At this time, we were looking for a similar area at Two Medicine to train new employees and sharpen the skills of the rest of us. Alas, every good place was either too inaccessible to use or too accessible to the public. What we finally came up with was usable but not like good old Wilbur Cliffs.

Any backcountry ranger at Glacier is bound to become familiar with toilet seats. The ones in the backcountry pit toilets tend to rust out and sliiiide - not a pleasant experience to users at home, let alone in the woods. As I perused my trail log for this time period, I ran across my comments about repainting these seats - a joyous and memorable job! Sometimes they prove to be unrepairable and have to be replaced. At Many Glacier, I carried one with the 'horseshoe' around my neck for about 4 miles - an experience that few people have known!

This illustrates the somewhat misleading nature of this book. It might seem that there was just one emergency after another (and occasionally this might have seemed to be true) but, in reality much of what we did was routine. To illustrate, I have enclosed a page of my personal patrol log (Appendix 2).

Speaking of my patrol log, there is a large gap in it starting at the end of July. The 29th of July proved to be one of the worst days of my life since I received word that my beloved mother lost her life in a traffic accident that day, almost 32 years after being permanently crippled in a previous one. The shock and grief was overwhelming. Thank God (literally!) for the Shewmakes. The whole family wrapped themselves around me with love. I actually slept in their apartment that night so as not to be alone in my trailer. Roger, Jean, and kids were totally sensitive to my situation. Roger paid for and made all of my travel arrangements home since I was almost totally dysfunctional at that time. I almost had to twist his arm later to find out the cost of the travel in order to pay them back.

The first accident was the result of an underage drunk driver on the wrong side of the road. On the second, a truck driver ran a stop sign. For a long time after this, I agonized over why this had happened to my family again. I didn't lose my faith but was very angry with God, and just wondered why. I have never received a definitive answer but have learned to accept this with the knowledge that she is in Heaven and able to walk, and even run, with two good legs.

I came back to Two Medicine just long enough to wrap things up, do one short patrol, and conduct a backcountry equipment orientation for a new employee. After arranging for the sale of my Apache trailer, I made a sad, lonely trip home.

Lake McDonald

Ranger Friends & Social Life

Regi Altop, Terry Spangler, Roger Shewmake

The Shewmake family (Roger, Jean, Sarah, & David),
The Schuster Family (Bob, Betty, Scott, & Ryan),
Altop & Spangler.

A ranger buffet; identifiable:
Dave Casteel, Roger Shewmake,
Bob Adams, & Betty Schuster.

GLACIER - 1987

I BEGAN 1987 with the hope that it would be better than the previous one. Once again there was no backcountry position open for my short season, but someone managed to jury-rig a position for me (full pay this time!) to utilize my bear management experience. Just as in the season before when I was a pioneer for armed VIP's, this season I was to be the one-and-only entrance station/bear management ranger! This was back at Two Medicine but was not my first experience in an entrance station. During my time at Many Glacier, I had spent a week or two in the entrance station kiosk covering for someone who had to leave early. My strongest memory from that experience was that the little building seemed to attract every fly in the world. I spent more time killing them than doing anything else! To this day, I believe entrance station rangers have the worst job in the NPS. You take people who by their very nature like the wide open spaces and put them in a box. It didn't help me that I am mildly claustrophobic anyway.

Nevertheless, I accepted the job in order to get back to Glacier in an actual paid position. The way that this strange combination of duties worked was this. If a bear situation arose for which I was needed, I would receive either a phone or radio call. Then I would put the closed sign up, grab the shotgun, which had been neatly tucked out of sight, and head out to deal with the situation. I, of course, had the .44 handgun in my pack. Little did the visitors know when they got in free that they had some bear to thank for it!

I believe it was around 25 June when I tried this procedure out for the first time. It was in response to a visitor report of a black bear sow with cubs near the North Shore trailhead. I found nothing, but while I was out there another visitor saw a black bear on the trail to Old Man Lake only about 100 yards away from me. Again, I found nothing. Statistically, black bears cause more injuries to people than grizzlies, but that is only because there are so many more black bears. When people encounter them, however, grizzlies are 30 times more likely to cause harm. Nevertheless, we take black bear encounters seriously, also.

On 1 July, was the next incident of note. Shewmake was patrolling the Old Man Lake Campground area which was closed because of grizzly activity at the time. Since we had been unable to reach him by radio, I headed into the area with revolver and shotgun. It was a relief when I contacted him about a half-mile beyond the Dry Fork Bridge. It turned out that he had been experiencing radio trouble and was delayed while clearing the area of visitors. In mountainous areas like Glacier, there are 'dead spots' in which radio transmission is difficult or impossible because of the terrain and/or atmospheric conditions. As we became familiar with the territory, we would start to become familiar with where those permanent 'dead spots' were. I don't remember whether Roger had a radio problem or a 'dead spot' problem in this case.

There is not much to say about the entrance station part of this job, but there is one note-worthy memory. The Blackfoot Indian Reservation borders the eastern boundary of Glacier, and each Sunday afternoon many of these folks would flock into Two Medicine for picnicking. Tribal membership ensured free entry. Some of these Blackfeet were Sunday afternoon regulars, and I got to know an elderly couple and befriended them. They gave me a great honor by inviting me to the Eagle ceremony in Browning, and I found it an interesting and worthwhile experience. A lot of American Indians try to retain many of their historical traditions, and this is one. Many stayed late on Sundays, and I can still remember listening to their drums at night and watching the smoke from their campfires drift up into the sky.

Next we will skip to the end of July because the interim time was mostly one of those routine periods that I have previously alluded to, with routine patrols and the swatting of flies at the entrance station.

25-27 July proved to be a period of high activity in the Two Med area. On the 25th, we received a report of an aggressive bear (species unknown) on the trail just above Appistoky Falls. Meanwhile, Shewmake was headed up to Upper Two Medicine Lake to close the trail between there and Twin Falls because of an aggressive grizzly on that trail. We were also dealing with a fire just south of the park boundary along Highway 2 (Circle the wagons!). I hiked out to check on the Appistoky Falls situation and checked out the trail and area well. I also interviewed about a dozen visitors who had been hiking in the area, but none had seen any sign of bears either going or coming- nor had I, so after about 2 hours of fruitless looking, I headed back and reached the station before 1600- another long day!

The 26th was routine enough until we received reports of possibly 2 aggressive grizzlies between Old Man Lake and the Dry Fork. Thus, I headed out on a bear patrol to warn campers not to go into the Old Man drainage. My particular assignment took me through the drainage between the two areas where the two bears in question had been observed. Unfortunately, the timetable involved didn't allow me to head out until 1900- near sunset. We tell visitors that hiking alone in grizzly country is not recommended- and especially at night. (The Blackfoot name for the grizzly means 'terrible night bear'!) Nevertheless, I was getting paid for this, so out I went.

Shewmake took me to the Prey Shelter by boat, and I hiked in from there. As if the gathering darkness wasn't bad enough, I ran into a brief thunder and hail storm on the way in and had to seek shelter under a tree until it subsided. In addition to making the appropriate notifications, I posted a sign at the Dawson Pass Trail junction, warning of the trail closure ahead. There are few places darker than the mountains during an overcast night, so on the way back out it was pitch black and a flashlight was required to follow the trail. My bear bells were jingling on my pack, and I was talking out loud to myself to make even more noise so as not to surprise any large furry critter. An amusing sidelight to this was that I had in my upper shirt pocket a small tape recorder which I had along to document any significant patrol observations. I decided to have it on during my return trip to record for posterity my conversation with myself. I still have that recording somewhere.

This round-trip hike was only about 5 miles, but it seemed to take forever before I reached the boat again at the Prey Shelter. Shewmake, Altop, and the park patrol boat were a sight for sore eyes!

This is a good time to talk a bit about how to behave in bear country. Both black and grizzly bears have what we call a 'personal space'. This is the space surrounding them, the entrance of which by another individual (such as a person) will cause the bear to feel threatened and to feel the need to take defensive action. This space can expand and contract, depending on the situation, the personality of the individual animals, or their particular mood at the time. Here are a couple of examples of this from each species. Once I encountered a black bear in the Many Glacier Campground. When I came within about 50 feet, it would take note of me and move slowly toward me. When I retreated out of that space, it began to ignore me again. As I moved back into the above-named space, I got the same reaction as before. This animal had a very well-defined personal space at that particular time. When I was in the Army in Alaska, while on a short off-duty trip to Denali National Park, I observed a grizzly along the park road, simply grazing on grass. It was drawing quite a crowd, all within 50-100 feet of the animal. In fact, a professional photographer actually began taking photos within only a few feet of the bear's head. Incredibly, this animal ignored it all. (Had I been a park ranger at the time, I would have whisked everyone away posthaste!) Only a short time later, with the photographer gone from in front of it, the bear became agitated by people much farther away. For reasons known only to the grizzly itself, its personal space had expanded dramatically.

The trick then is to let the bear know of your presence before you get into its space. By making a lot of noise before that happens, the bear is able to move away and recreate that space again before the person enters it. With black bears this is not quite as important since they often take defensive action by simply climbing a tree. It is more important with grizzlies, however, since the adults normally can't or won't climb trees. They therefore sometimes feel the need to defend themselves on the ground by charging when surprised. Thus, making noise is important to make the animals aware of your presence before they feel threatened. Bears have hearing about like ours and, I believe, better eyesight than they are given credit for, but their sense of smell is outstanding and what they rely most heavily on. As a result of this, if the wind is at your back, it is not likely that you would surprise one. With the wind in your face is when the noise-making becomes particularly important. For myself, I would normally have 2 'bear bells' attached to my pack, of two different sizes. These are actually cow bell-like in design. For routine patrol situations and the wind at my back, I would have only the smaller one out. With the wind wrong and/or fresh bear sign, I would use both together. My expression on the radio in such situations was "It's getting to be a two-bell day!"

Since bears don't normally charge large groups of people, I usually only have used the small bell when leading a group of visitors or traveling with a group of friends. (I personally don't know of any case where a group of 5 or more people has been charged.) I believe that this is because the more people there are, the more human scent there is, the more noise they produce, and the more dominant and formidable they seem to be. We call this 'pulling dominance'. Although the advice to make plenty of noise on the trail is sound, it is sometimes unrealistic because people forget, especially when they are huffing and puffing up and down hill. The use of bells have come into disrepute because too many people were using the little 'jingle bells' which aren't nearly loud enough, and simply give a sense of false security. I can't count the number of times that I have come around the blind corner of a trail and encountered someone with these small bells that I saw before I ever heard them. The same could have happened with a bear.

The recommendation of choice today is pepper spray - like mailmen carry. They are 70-80+ % effective in turning bear charges, but there are problems with this also. If the wind is in the person's face, which would often be the situation with a surprised bear, the spray may actually blow back into their face and disable the person rather than the animal. The spray has a limited range and duration and a panicky user can exhaust it before the animal comes in range. My personal preference is to carry both the spray AND the bells. In fact, I was one of the early carriers of the spray when it first came into vogue.

Anyway, I digress. The next day it was back to Old Man Lake - this time to give an armed escort to some campers coming out of the closed area. This time, at least, it was in daylight. One of the 4 people in the campground was NPS naturalist, Don Halloran. He and his companion were eye witnesses to the bear incident the day before, and they headed into Pitamakin Pass to be interviewed by Roger Shewmake who was putting a closure sign there. I escorted the other 2 out. It was as hot a day and hike as I have ever experienced in the park, made especially long by the bad knee of one of my charges. We saw no further evidence of fresh bear activity.

On 5 August, Bob Isdahl, Roger Shewmake, and I headed to the west side for an all-day training course called 'Helispot Managing, I-272. This involved learning how to direct helicopters in for landings and also how to direct their takeoffs - another certificate and another skill to add to the resume.

It is always nice to have visits from friends. On 7 August, I was visited by friends from my home town and home church - the Maag family. We hiked, picnicked, and went on a boat trip back at my old stomping ground at Many Glacier. I enjoyed their visit immensely, and I believe that they had a good time also.

Most of the rest of my summer was spent manning the entrance kiosk and doing routine backcountry patrols. I was also frantically trying to finish mapping backcountry emergency helispots. Before I left, Shewmake and I tried to locate every possible landing site in the sub-district. This would hopefully prevent any difficult situations like we had with the backcountry cardiac incident the year before. This turned out to earn me a Special Achievement Award for developing this backcountry evacuation system. There was a cash award with this and, of course, a significant chunk of it was withheld for taxes.

The only other items of note were a belaying and rapelling training session for new employees in which I assisted Roger Shewmake in instructing on 21 August. My very last patrol was on 1 September, checking out a report of a grizzly in the Running Eagle Falls area. I found no bear but posted the trail with a 'Grizzly Frequenting' sign anyway.

Before I left for the season, I had a conversation with Dallas Koehn, East Side District Ranger. The park was trying to get all of the backcountry/bear management rangers commissioned as law enforcement rangers. There had been some serious bear incidents over the recent seasons and an increased emphasis was being placed on backcountry rules enforcement, particularly in terms of food storage. When those of us without commissions encountered violations in the backcountry, we had to radio back and have a commissioned ranger ready to meet us at the trailhead as we escorted the violator out. Dallas told me that if I got my commission I could name my job for the coming season. This gave me a lot of food for thought as I drove back to Illinois.

Glacier Rangers in the Backcountry:

Shewmake - working on a bear pole.

Altop - resting during boundary patrol

Spangler, repairing a backcountry pit toilet door.

Routine Duties

Spangler on a boundary patrol

Canoe patrol with Altop in the bow (shown) and Spangler in the stern (not shown).

Terry Spangler - doing repairs at Lee Creek Cabin.

Glacier Wildlife

Coyote

Bull elk

Golden Eagle

Pink spiraea - one of more than 1000 species of wild flowers growing in Glacier.

NATIONAL RANGER TRAINING INSTITUTE – 1988

ALTHOUGH I HAD decided to follow Dallas Koehn's advice, I had to somehow work it into my schedule. The seasonal law enforcement schools approved and authorized by the government lasted 6 weeks, and therefore, the school year was out. The only time that I could match my schedule to theirs was the summer, and that meant taking the summer off from the NPS - sort of like taking a step back in order to take 2 steps forward. There were several of these schools around the country, and after researching them, I applied to and was accepted at The National Ranger Training Institute, affiliated with Hocking Technical College in Nelsonville, Ohio. This school offered a number of ranger-related courses - everything from EMS to horsemanship. I only took the law enforcement one, however. This course ran from 29 June through 11 August and was supposed to be for 260 hours but actually ran close to 285 hours.

This proved to be the hottest summer that I can ever remember in the Midwest with day after endless day over 100 degrees, and humidity to match. The school officials seemed to be trying to find out who was serious about this, because for the first week or two classes were conducted in a classroom with no air conditioning, no windows, and little ventilation. It was brutal! Few if any dropped out though. I stayed in my pickup camper in the school campground, saving a lot of money. I also had access to the nearby school locker room shower facilities. Mercifully, my camper air conditioner worked marvelously all summer, and this made my humble abode a great refuge from the heat.

The subject matter was very intense and included a generous mix of both classroom and hands-on subjects and activities. Subjects included such things as Constitutional law, search & seizure, arrest procedures, narcotics & drug enforcement, bombs & explosives, among others in a classroom setting. Hands-on activities included such things as defensive tactics, defensive driving, and firearms training. A subject that would cure anybody's insomnia is traffic enforcement. A seemingly endless amount of time was spent on it.

The big emphasis was on handgun proficiency, however. The shooting instructors there were excellent, and I didn't realize how many pistol shooting flaws that I had until I received this instruction. Classroom sessions were normally of the 8AM - 5PM variety, but the firearms sessions were sometimes lasting as long as 14 hours. Not only that, but there were no lunch breaks on the range or any water breaks. This was especially brutal in the intense heat. We had to bring our own food and water and find time to eat and drink when another group was on the firing line.

The defensive tactics sessions were sometimes brutal also. Curiously enough, there was no baton training, although there was a separate baton course that could be taken. Virtually everything involved fighting with our hands and feet, and some of it was quite intense. One of the instructors taught the hands-and-feet fighting, and the other one taught some judo skills. Everything got hot and physical - especially demanding with the ever present heat. Some members of past classes had suffered injuries, but ours escaped relatively unscathed, though one of our number was slammed to the gym floor by the instructor when caught unawares (with no gym mat underneath, by the way). We were certainly learning to always be alert - especially when the judo guy moved behind us!

The main routine was to pair off and take turns practicing strikes, kicks, and take-down procedures. The partner receiving the blows used football blocking dummies for protection. One bizarre, but useful, drill was to practice fighting in a confined space. To do this we had to fight our way into and out of a restroom toilet stall by fighting through the partner who was to vigorously resist with a hand dummy. Again, the heat took its toll. My partner happened to be a former college football lineman from Miami of Ohio and outweighed me by 50 or 60 pounds. This may seem unfair but you don't get to pick your opponent in real life either. The school concluded with both day and night scenarios.

I was fortunate enough to finish number #1 in the class, but had an unfair advantage since I was the only one with previous Park Service experience. This actually allowed me to make the college dean's list - a new experience for me! To summarize, the school had a good reputation going in and it didn't disappoint.

Next to come, when I got home - the confirmed bachelor (me) was getting married to a very special woman named Julie.

NATIONAL

Ranger

TRAINING INSTITUTE

.....a federal law enforcement
training site which includes...

.....defensive driving......

.....classroom work.

..frisking & handcuffing..

...traffic direction training..

.....and gas attack training.

Pictured Rocks Natl. Lakeshore - 1989

Successfully completing law enforcement school does not actually result in a law enforcement commission - rather it simply makes a person 'commissionable'. Only the park that hires the ranger can commission them. Therefore, I was all dressed for the party and was looking to find out where it would be. I had assumed that I would be going back to Glacier since that was my motivation for going to law enforcement school in the first place. Ironically, the fact that I now was to have a commission meant that I had to commit to a full 6 months as a commissioned Glacier backcountry/bear management ranger. I obviously couldn't work for that extended time period. I could have gotten another position there, but then would have wasted the time, effort, and expense of the previous summer. (Some NPS training is at government expense - this was not.) Thus, Glacier was not to be the 'party' that I was dressed for.

I ended up taking a position at Pictured Rocks National Lakeshore in Michigan. It is in a rugged part of the Upper Peninsula bordering the south shore of Lake Superior. It covers more than 70,000 acres of multi-colored cliffs, broad beaches, sand dunes, waterfalls, ponds, and forests.

The job matched my skill set well and involved basically being in charge of all activities in my part of the park. I could basically make out my own schedule in managing a campground, conducting backcountry and road patrols, and providing EMS. I even conducted an evening campfire program on Thursday nights.

After the Yellowstone fires of the previous year, all of the park areas were mandated to select a ranger to explain NPS fire management policy periodically to visitors. I was selected for that task at Pictured Rocks, and I used my campfire program to do that. The Chief Interpreter did not want me to give the program while armed so I would simply come off of road patrol, leave my handgun in the vehicle, start the fire and present the hour-long program.

As to the law enforcement, this first season was the smoothest transition that I have ever had. Since I had graduated from LE school less than a year before, most of the normal pre-season requirements could be omitted. Normally, a 40-hour refresher course was required every year as well as a firearms recertification before commissioning could take place, but I had already done both within the year. Therefore, it was smooth sailing into the commission and the job. I had technically become a Type II Government Security Specialist or what is more commonly called a Type II Law Enforcement Ranger or, simply, a seasonal law enforcement ranger. Type I rangers are permanent and work year round. They usually start as seasonals and apply for permanent status. This involves attending FLETCE (the Federal Law Enforcement Training Center) in Glenco, Georgia. The main difference between the two, other than the additional schooling, is that a Type II LE cannot lead an investigation. Only Type I rangers are allowed to do that, but Type II rangers may assist in those investigations.

This is perhaps a good place to comment briefly that all divisions of the Park Service have both seasonal and permanent employees. We seasonals are sort of the 'Army Reserve' of the National Park Service. We are hired to work in times of maximum visitation. When I was at Glacier, for instance, there were approximately 360 employees in the summer but in the winter, with most of the roads closed by snow, there would be only the 60 or so permanent employees. The average summer visitor would likely encounter only seasonal workers. On the other hand, parks with relatively consistent year- round visitation, or very little visitation, may employ no seasonals at all. It is all about the needs of the particular park area and the available funds.

Anyway, back to Pictured Rocks. As I said, this job was right up my alley. The only real set-in-stone structure, other than the Thursday night campfire program, was collecting and processing the campground remit every Friday. The processing was done at headquarters, and this was normally the only time that I was back in civilization during the work week.

Although the job was fine, the location and living conditions were not. The Sullivan Creek cabin had only intermittent electricity because it ran off of a generator, and the propane fuel was very expensive to buy and to haul. To make matters worse, it was all at my expense. There was running water, but hot water also required the generator. The cabin was about a 45 minute drive from the nearest small town, and the road was pure sand and dirt. I don't remember any smooth areas on it. There was just one pothole after another! This might have been problematic enough when I was a single ranger, because the road was very hard on vehicles, but I now had a wife with two step children along, and this whole primitive package was very difficult for them. They made the best of it, however.

Although there were 2 auto campgrounds in my area of the park, the remoteness of the area and the poor road conditions meant that we had relatively light visitation. This made for a light law enforcement load, which was fortunate since I was a rookie at this aspect of park work. Also, any backup I might request would probably be miles away. I probably couldn't contact them anyway since there were so many radio 'dead spots' in the area. This rookie cop was truly on his own!

Because I patrolled 2 vehicle campgrounds, most of the violations I dealt with were minor camping ones, normally involving just warnings. I did, however, issue my first ever citation in early August and only one other the rest of the summer - both camping violations. My only real encounter with animals involved a number of dogs off of leash in the campground. Only one of those was noteworthy. As I recall, it was a German Shepard who started to approach me menacingly as I entered the owner's campsite. I shouted to this owner in no uncertain terms that if he didn't get the dog under physical restraint immediately, I would shoot him. Needless to say, the compliance was immediate!

There are black bears in Pictured Rocks, but our only encounter with any occurred one night when my wife apparently encountered one near the front door of the cabin. This was probably a young and curious one which showed no aggressiveness. The irony was that I had originally become a federal cop to do bear management, and I did none here.

I received a good job evaluation, but I worked so independently and remotely that I seldom saw a supervisor, so I don't know how they could rate me at all. I guess that they were just being generous! So ended my season at Pictured Rocks.

1990 was another stay-at-home summer to conduct other business.

Panorama

Sullivan Creek Ranger Cabin

Au Sable Light Station

Munising Falls

Spangler, conducting campfire program.

Crater Lake Natl. Park - 1991

ONE OF THE job offers that I received for the 1991 season was from Crater Lake National Park. This was particularly intriguing since they bragged that they had the best seasonal housing in the Park Service, including married housing. Thus, we headed for Oregon. The housing claim turned out to be true. We were assigned a delightful cabin, one of the so-called stone cottages. It had all of the modern conveniences that a family could want and was situated in a little ranger village with other seasonals. This was a law enforcement position, however, so before settling in it was necessary for us to head to Redwoods National Park in northern California for my 40 hour LE refresher course.

As I mentioned earlier, this had not been necessary at Pictured Rocks since I had finished the full course within the year. The refreshers are always sort of a "Readers' Digest" version of the original course. What stood out in my first refresher ever was the emphasis on the proper use of deadly force. The firearms qualification was also more realistic with more combat-like shooting, including practicing shooting past a hostage to take out a hostage taker. Somehow the word got around that I was a Special Achievement Award winner, and that was the first time that I was aware that it wasn't often given, especially to seasonals.

It was nice to see Redwoods and experience our first ever trip to California, but now it was on to Crater Lake for the summer. I had an interesting experience as my supervisor, Doug Raeburn, was introducing me to other members of the team. Upon meeting me, fellow patrol ranger Mark Seeley commented," Gosh, I thought you'd be bigger!" I took this as a complement but didn't know for sure why he said it. As I said, our quarters were the best we have ever experienced in the NPS but, in early June, it was still partially buried in snow. We could actually walk up to the second floor window from the outside, and it wasn't until the 4th of July that we could actually get our back door open!

Before proceeding, let's look at the lay of the land at Crater Lake. The park was created to preserve a deep blue lake formed by the collapse of an ancient volcano called Mt. Mazama. This collapse caused the formation of a caldera which filled with water, forming a lake that is almost 2000 feet deep, the deepest in the U.S.A. It contains some of the purest and least polluted water in the world. The surface area of the whole park covers about 183,000 acres in southern Oregon. A 33 mile paved road circles the caldera and presents many scenic views. 57 miles south lies Klamath Falls - the nearest town. It is this remoteness that makes the in-park housing so important.

The remoteness also makes the necessity for a modern, well-equipped ambulance important. This was the first place that I had worked that we had one like this. I was soon to find out how important it was. Our normal procedure when we made an ambulance run was to meet a Klamath Falls ambulance halfway and make a patient transfer. This was necessary because we only had one vehicle, and we didn't want it to be too far away for too long. This meant that we didn't always know the final outcome for the patient. That was a little frustrating, but the necessity of this became apparent when we had just come back from a run one time and were still cleaning up the vehicle when we received another ambulance call. In fact, we once had 3 calls the same day. The main reason for this is that many people take the Cleetwood Trail which is the only access to the lake and, thus, the only way to reach the tour boat. Obviously, the lake itself is the main focal point in the park and, therefore, many people opt to take the boat. Although the Cleetwood Trail is only a mile long, it is quite steep all the way and is, of course, at altitude. It is all downhill to the boat, but what goes down must come up, and a lot of people are not prepared for that high altitude, mile-long hike in thin air. In fact, this particular summer I probably dealt with more EMS responses than in any other park that I worked.

At first, my LE road patrols were ride alongs with other rangers who were more familiar with the territory. My first solo was on 26 June, according to my own patrol log. It was uneventful.

A rash of lockouts occurred in those early days, and I am no whiz with a 'slim jim' (used to slide inside the car window to spring the latch). The most difficult are the electronic locks which are very challenging because there is no external button to engage. On one of these that I had on a cold day up the mountain, I patiently explained to the unfortunate owner that I was unlikely to get in and that we would probably have to call a professional locksmith from quite a ways off. I said that I would give it a shot, however. I almost immediately engaged the inner release and the door was open. I think the guy thought that I was some kind of miracle worker, but little did he know that it was simply blind luck!

On the evening of 8 July, we received a report of a case of drunk and disorderly in a concession dorm. The word came back that he wished to fight a cop. What made matters more ominous was he was built like, and had the size of, an NFL linebacker. This was where my combination law enforcement/EMS skill set came in handy. I simply made contact with him as an EMT, complete with medical jump kit. This worked well in calming him down, and he allowed me to treat him. I also confiscated some drug paraphernalia and marijuana residue. Now comes probably the stupidest thing I have ever done in law enforcement. Later, in checking out the evidence in our evidence locker, I realized it (the marijuana bong) was not there. To my horror, I realized that I had failed to secure it from the suspect! So much for chain of evidence! I quickly returned to his room and, fortunately, found and secured all of it. Since the amount of marijuana was minimal I gave him a $275.00 citation, and that was the end of it.

The next day, 9 July, brought another medical call, this time to the Cleetwood Cove Trail. Oxygen was the treatment necessary. As I said before, that trail is no picnic for a lot of folks. The 10th was the 3rd day in a row with a medical, this time for a temporary blackout in the Mazama Campground. I checked back with this individual a couple of days later and everything was A-O.K. Altitude can affect even healthy people in negative ways until they get used to it. It usually takes me about 2 weeks to totally acclimatize when coming from the 'flatlands'.

Although Type II law enforcement rangers can assist with investigations, they are not supposed to lead them. Sometimes personnel limitations dictate otherwise, however. 18 July was one of those times. The boat concession spilled gasoline into the lake, and this was particularly serious considering the pristine nature of the lake water. I was assigned to conduct the investigation. I conducted a number of taped interviews with concession employees, but they were all deaf and dumb. No one admitted to knowing anything. They were circling the wagons around the company, and there were no other witnesses that I could locate who would admit to witnessing this environmental violation. One employee even asked to be read his Miranda Rights before being questioned, which I did. An interesting sidelight was that this particular employee was my wife Julie's boss. This happened to be the only time she worked a summer for the concessionaires. Her position was stocking groceries in the gift shop and campground store. Although it was a good summer for both of us, the job was sometimes uncomfortable for her. She sometimes had to work with people that I had issued a citation or warning to the day before or, as just stated, interviewed in a criminal investigation. To conclude, we had hoped to take this case to the grand jury, but we could find no cooperative witnesses. Some concession person(s) were fired, however - I think because of the spill.

Each LE ranger was given a special project in addition to regular duties. Since I was the only ranger at Crater Lake with experience with bears, I became the one and only bear management ranger there. So, for the first time since going to law enforcement school, precisely in order to do bear management, I was finally doing bear management! There are no grizzlies in the park - only black bears, and very few problems with them at the time. Thus, my duties in this regard were primarily limited to getting a bear culvert trap repaired and rehabilitated.

19 July started off routinely enough, with routine paperwork and a routine patrol followed by gas spill investigative work, which was still going on at the time. Before lunch, I checked out a report of cattle in the park, but found no sign of any.

After lunch nothing was routine, and it became one of those "circle the wagons" type of days. First, we answered a medical emergency call at Rim Village. After returning from that, Chief Ranger George Buckingham hollered down from his second story office that he wanted me to come in and brief him on the progress of the gas spill investigation. Just as he said that, someone thrust a crumbled up piece of paper into my hand. It said, "armed motorcyclist in the visitor center". I got LE ranger Mark Magnuson as backup and headed for the VC. The personnel there said that he was in the theater watching the orientation video. After finding out how much time was left on the film, Mark and I stepped outside to formulate a game plan. I asked him if he had his ballistic vest on. He did not, and I did, so I was elected to be the contact person and he would be the cover. We stood outside and waited for the guy to come out. We positioned ourselves so as not to be detected until he cleared the door. As he came out, I moved up behind him and said, "Park ranger - don't move!" At the same time, I reached into his shoulder holster and removed a loaded Army .45 caliber handgun. I quickly unloaded it and handed it to Magnuson. The situation turned out to be less ominous than it first appeared. The guy was a 60+ year old gentleman traveling with his wife from their Arizona home where open firearms carry is permitted, and we took his word that he didn't know our rules. (Firearms at that time had to be unloaded and cased or broken down while in a national park area.) After a verbal warning, we sent him on his way with the unloaded and properly stashed gun.

On 23 July, I experienced a hair raising car chase. At 1030, while on road patrol, I was on a part of our road system in which commercial traffic was forbidden. I encountered a semi and switched on my lights and siren. Instead of stopping he sped up. Our respective speeds reached 75 miles per hour as he tried to beat me to the park boundary. This was unacceptable speed on a winding mountain road, and to make matters worse, there was significant road construction just outside the park. I considered contacting law enforcement outside the park to intercept but decided the risk of a semi barreling through construction and construction workers was just not worth the risk, so I gave up and broke off contact. Sometimes in a case of 'fish or cut bait' it is best to cut bait!

I caught up with a lot of wrong-doers that summer, however, including a citation for illegal camping that afternoon. Actually, I issued more citations that summer than any other one, and the majority were for illegal camping. One of our maintenance employees actually remarked that I was the most intimidating cop that he had ever seen. (Gosh, at least my wife loves me!) In fact, one of my most embarrassing moments occurred in one of these incidents. Doug Raeburn and I found an illegal camp that had been occupied by a young couple who worked for the concession company. After issuing the citation, we went through the standard procedure of inventorying personal property from the camp back to these two owners. Among the 'very personal' property was a used male protection device (to use the most dignified possible term for it!). Doug and I maintained as much dignity as possible in returning it! I think that we were almost as embarrassed as the 'perpetrators'!

I mentioned earlier that I gave out more citations this particular summer than in any other, but I actually gave even more warnings. The sequence for this at the time was verbal warning, written warning, and violation notice. Everything is still the same except that the written warning at that time was called a 'courtesy tag'. That term has been dropped, perhaps because it appeared a little too friendly, but I actually don't know the reason. Nevertheless, it was up to our discretion as to which one we gave. For minor violations in which the person seemed to have transgressed without knowing it, or the violation was exceedingly minor, I would normally give a warning. If, however, I deemed the person to know better, it was a major violation, or the person was a repeat offender, it was time to lighten their pocketbook!

Statistically, car stops are one of the most dangerous law enforcement response situations that there are, 2nd only to domestic disputes. In national parks, the most obvious locations for these disputes are in campgrounds. This was not the location for such a domestic dispute at Crater Lake on 29 July, however. I came on duty at 1500 since I had the 'graveyard shift' that day. At 1700 we received a report at headquarters about this particular domestic issue on Wizard Island, a volcanic cone that rises up from the surface of Crater Lake itself. The scenario went like this: A group of scientists from Oregon State University had a permit to do research on the island and were in the middle of a week-long campout there. The estranged wife of one of the professors became convinced that her professor husband was having an "orgy" there with a lady professor. The concession tour boat made regular stops out there, and the wife took one of the tours out to confront them. When the boat was ready to leave, she refused to get back on and leave the island. She would hurl volcanic rocks and cinders at anyone who tried to get her aboard. John Broward and I were elected to go and fetch her. Before going, we were able to get a phone call in to her daughter to get a handle on her emotional state. She indicated that her mother was delusional and could be violent. Radio calls from the island also indicated that she was threatening suicide by throwing herself into the lake. As John and I headed out there, we formed a game plan. As is always the case, we would interview the couple separately. On the trip back, we couldn't use handcuffs, because if she somehow managed to jump out of the park patrol boat, she would surely drown. We decided that we would put her between us on the boat - me on the left and John on the right. Being left-handed, that put my handgun side away from her and the same with right-handed John on the other side.

When we got there she was still pretty well wound up but her actions had turned from violence to whimpering and crying. Broward interviewed her, and I interviewed the husband. The general consensus was that nothing romantic had occurred on the island. We were able to get her on the boat without resistance. On the cruise back she was very depressed, and we kept alert for any attempt at a jump into the drink. None occurred. To assure that she didn't try to bolt away while climbing the Cleetwood Cove Trail, we stayed close and set a fast pace so that she became too exhausted to run. She was transferred to psychiatric care outside the park, and we could then breathe a sigh of relief. Our part was done, but unfortunately, we never heard what became of her.

At Glacier, when off duty, we did not have to stay in the area, or even in the park. Nevertheless, if we were in the area, it was expected that we would respond to any emergency that we were aware of. At Crater Lake, however, I had my first and only experience of being on call. True, I have had that duty as a volunteer EMT at home, but only once in the Park Service - at Crater Lake. Each of the law enforcement personnel took their regular turn at this, and we would occasionally be called out. The difference between this and regular off duty was that we were required to be in the area with our radio on. I just mention this in passing.

On 5 August, one of the most memorable events I have ever experienced in the Park Service, or for that matter, in my whole life occurred. It was about 2200 hours, and I was working the late shift. As I cruised through the Rim Village area, I saw a car in the parking lot. Since overnight parking was not allowed there, I got on the intercom and informed them that they could not stay. I saw heads bob up above the seats and duck back down and they appeared to be sacking out. I decided to run a background check on the license plate. I called it in to our dispatch in Medford. It came back as a stolen vehicle. I got on the intercom again and said," All occupants exit the vehicle please!" Instead of exiting, they headed the car down the mountain to the south. As I left in pursuit, I notified dispatch of the chase. I also called John Broward who was patrolling in that direction. Somewhere out there in the dark, John began setting up a road block.

As the speed picked up while heading down this winding mountain road, I began to have the same feeling that I had while pursuing the semi driver. This was no place for a high speed chase. I could visualize some unsuspecting approaching vehicle - so I slowed down, knowing that the roadblock was somewhere ahead.

Then something strange happened. As I slowed down, they slowed down. When I speeded up, they speeded up, always keeping 50-100 yards between us. When we reached the turnoff into the administration loop, they turned in. I pulled my vehicle up to block the only way out. I thought that now we had them trapped. The problem was that the park housing area, including my own family dwelling, was only a 100 yards or so away. I didn't want to see them fleeing on foot into the housing complex, starting a gun fight, or creating a hostage situation. Hopefully, all of the doors were locked! While spinning a lot of things through my mind, another unexpected thing happened. They whipped around the circle and headed straight for me, and it looked like I was about to be t-boned. Worse, I was silhouetted sideways in their headlights with the most vulnerable part of my ballistic vest toward them - the seam down the side. Thus, I backed in the direction opposite the road block which guided them toward it. John had set it up only a short distance down the road, and still in the residential area. Thus, we now had them bottled up.

When the suspect vehicle reached the roadblock, I withdrew the shotgun from the gunlock and covered them across the engine block. Again, I got on the intercom and instructed the occupants to exit. As I did this, I gratefully noticed that there were no visitors around to complicate the issue. Then, suddenly, there appeared a whole line of cars behind Broward's vehicle and another line behind me. It reminded me of the last scene of the movie "Field of Dreams"! All of a sudden, a man in Bermuda shorts walked up beside me and asked if I needed any help. I told him in no uncertain terms to move back. I got on the intercom again and asked all visitors to "exit the area, please". I repeated this and nothing happened. Finally, I simply said "All visitors - scram!" This plain language did work and the headlights slowly began moving and melted into the night.

In the meantime, two occupants did hesitantly get out of the suspect car and, after significant urging, followed my instructions and went face down on the pavement with their arms straight out and their legs crossed. At about this time supervisory ranger Doug Raeburn came out of the woods to assist. He had been alerted to this incident and had pulled on his vest while hurrying to the scene. He made contact at the vehicle while John and I acted as cover officers. I knew that we were dealing with at least two individuals, and it turned out that was all there were when Doug examined the vehicle. While Raeburn was doing this, a disconcerting thing happened.

One of the suspects began moving his hand slowly towards his body. They had not been frisked yet, and Doug had his back turned to them while only a few feet away at the car. I warned the guy to move his hand back from his body. There was no compliance. I then told him that if he continued to move his hand toward his body, I would kill him where he lay! When he still didn't move his hand away from a possible weapon, I tried to 'pull more dominance' (i.e. intimidate him into compliance) by saying

"I have a shotgun, and if you don't move your hand back, I'm going to open you up like a ripe watermelon!" My finger had slipped inside the trigger guard and was lightly touching the trigger. Thoughts were quickly whirling through my mind. How long should I wait? His hand was only a short distance from a possible concealed handgun. In a second or two, he could have it out and have a point blank shot at Raeburn from the back. If he continued to reach toward his body, and I shot him, and he turned out not to have a weapon, I would have killed an unarmed man. On the other hand, if he quickly draws a gun and shoots Doug, how do I tell his wife that she is a widow because I couldn't pull the trigger in time? A quick decision had to be made - what do I do!?

Mercifully, and I believe by the Grace of God, the hand moved back into the spread eagle position. We had run the plate again and, once again it came back as a stolen vehicle. Also, the registration came back to a professor from the University of Oregon. We called him and found out that he had loaned his car to these two individuals for a trip to Crater Lake. They were exchange students from Japan, and they were not armed. A whole series of circumstances led to the events that I have been describing,

First, some dispatcher in Medford had hit the wrong button triggering the stolen vehicle report and then, incredibly, did it again when we checked in to verify. The two students were not fluent in English, and when I told them to 'exit the vehicle', they thought I meant to exit WITH the vehicle. They therefore believed me to be escorting them down the mountain. Thus, this explained their careful attempt to maintain the interval between our vehicles. Adding to their confusion was the fact that I was driving a patrol car with subdued identification (i.e. The flashers were in the grill). They were not used to that in Japan. We were able to get their version of events by dragging out of bed the only employee at Crater Lake who spoke Japanese and could interpret. They were having a hard time understanding my instructions because of the language barrier, but when the one individual saw the shotgun, he indicated that it motivated him to move his hand back away from his body. I have a different take on that, however. I believe that the good Lord interceded to keep me from killing an innocent person.

In retrospect, the whole event was surreal. Our flashing lights seemed to be everywhere, and my intercom instructions were echoing off of the surrounding mountains. To make matters more confusing, I was using 3 microphones as I was covering the suspects. One was the intercom, another was on local to my 2 compatriots, and the 3rd was hitting the repeater to the Medford dispatch. As I reached for them while trying to keep my eyes on the seemingly not-too-cooperative suspects, I sometimes grabbed the wrong one. Thus, all of the police radios in a good part of Oregon were hearing me threaten to 'open them up like a ripe watermelon' and possibly even with the echoes! The new seasonal housing called Sleepy Hollow had a balcony that overlooked the scene and the occupants got quite a show. All that was missing was theater popcorn!

We ended up escorting the two shook up visitors to our nearby campground for a peaceful remainder of the night. Our incident debriefing occurred just afterward, at 0200, about 4 hours after the beginning of the incident. What still chills me to the bone is the evaluation of my performance by my superiors. They said that I had done everything right. This was unsettling. If I had made a significant mistake, I could have assured myself that such an event would not happen again because I would be careful not to make that mistake again, but in this case there was nothing for me to correct. The only mistake had been made by a dispatcher who hit a wrong button in Medford - twice! The irony of that is, of all of the dispatch services that I have ever dealt with, the Medford dispatchers are the best that I have ever worked with. They were dedicated, conscientious, and extremely professional in every way - but anyone can make mistakes. Perhaps Chief Ranger George Buckingham summed it up best when he said," Sometimes these things happen."- very true, but not very comforting!

As I write this, police officers are under siege in this country for using what some people think is excessive force. In a few cases that may be true. I have occasionally worked with rangers who were overly aggressive. (We called them 'heat seekers'.) They were rare, however. Most of the people I have worked with have been conscientious and sincerely just trying to do their job the best way that they knew how. It is easy to be a 'Monday morning quarterback' in critiquing the actions of officers when deadly force is involved. Critics have hours, days or weeks to judge the action while we may have only seconds, or even split-seconds to make life/death decisions. Mercifully, things turned out o.k. in my case, and I credit the Good Lord above for that!

The next couple of days were filled with a variety of routine things - from the ever present government paperwork to a tick removal, a disabled vehicle, and a lockout. Then on 8 August, the next true emergency occurred. At 1645, Mark Magnuson and I responded to a medical call in the Rim Village Parking lot. It turned out to be a diabetic lady with hypoglycemia and in the early stages of insulin shock. We administered glucose gel but found the victim to be somewhat uncooperative. We recommended ambulance transfer to the hospital. The family completely concurred, but the patient would have none of it. Insulin shock can prove fatal rather quickly, and medical transport was certainly indicated, but any rational adult has the right to refuse. Mark and I conferred with the family, and we decided to do something that I had never done before, or since. We declared implied consent. This can be used to make a decision for an unconscious or mentally incapacitated patient. This individual was obviously deteriorating both mentally and physically. Thus, we considered this a possible life/death situation that trumped the liability risk to us.

As I recall, it was the Klamath Falls ambulance that we made the transfer to at about the halfway mark to the hospital. The patient was not improved at the transfer, and we never did hear about the outcome. This is always frustrating when you don't hear about the end result.

We got back just in time for me to deal with a visitor's injured knee, a disabled vehicle, and a possible lost/stolen wallet with credit card misuse.

The next day, I made a decision that I still regret. I was on patrol on the Rim Drive checking out a possible smoke (wildfire) when I noticed a dog off leash at a pullout. I didn't stop at that time because I was focused on checking out the possible fire. This turned out to be simply low-hanging clouds. On the way back, I noticed the same vehicle in the same pullout. A lady was there in great distress. The dog I had seen, a beautiful Irish setter, had chased a ground squirrel over the rim and fallen over the cliff. Her husband had scrambled down to rescue the dog and could not get back up. A rescue team was called in, and the man was brought up unhurt by a technical rescue. The dog was a different story. It did not survive the fall. I tried to console the couple, but they were inconsolable - so much for a happy vacation. We were sensitive in allowing a dignified burial in the park. I couldn't help but second guess myself in not stopping and assuring that the dog was put under restraint when I first saw it. This illustrates one reason why we require that pets be under restraint in national parks. Also, they are out of their normal surroundings and can stress the local wildlife as well as pass and receive diseases. I personally recommend that they be left at home with appropriate caretakers.

The rest of my short summer was taken up with routine traffic violations, the ever present government paperwork, and a couple of not-so-routine medicals - one involving possible kidney stones and another, a possible cardiac problem on the 15th. Before taking leave of Crater Lake, however, there is one incident I would like to take note of. We sometimes joke about making a top ten list of weird visitors that we have encountered in the parks. I have to mention one that we encountered at Crater Lake that certainly makes my list. For about a week or more (I don't remember precisely how long) a man would come into the visitor center at 0830, sit down and stare at our lady workers until 1030 and then leave. He never took his eyes off of them, and they understandably found this very unnerving. We didn't have any loitering regulations, so we really couldn't do anything. He drove a white station wagon with North Dakota plates. We also began to get reports that he was relieving himself along the road, partly out of sight in the woods. While we were trying to determine whether he was far enough into the woods to claim privacy, or whether he was guilty of indecent exposure, he disappeared as suddenly as he had appeared.

All that was left to do before leaving for the season was to make sure that the bear trap was fully operational. Then it was off to Illinois.

Top: The Spangler residence at Crater Lake
Middle: Golden-mantled Ground Squirrel - a
familiar sight along the rim
Bottom: Wizard Island in Crater Lake

Upper left: The Pinnacles

Upper right: The Phantom Ship

Bottom: Vidae Falls

SAGUARO NATL. MONUMENT – 1993

WE WERE MOVING again in 1992, so I took another season off. 1993 was unique right from the start. For all of my interest in National Park Service areas, I had never heard of Saguaro National Monument (now Saguaro National Park). Thus, I never applied there for the 1993 season. Nevertheless, I received a job offer from them out of the clear blue! I had never received a job offer before for a position for which I had not applied. I didn't even think that the NPS could do that - but there it was. It was a law enforcement position, and I ended up accepting it.

Saguaro National Monument was established in 1933 to protect a segment of the Sonoran Desert and the saguaro cactuses for which this park area is named. It is actually divided into eastern and western districts, on either side of the city of Tucson, Arizona. The two areas together comprise about 84,000 acres. I was actually hired to work in the Saguaro East District, also called the Rincon Mountain District (RMD). The other is called the Saguaro West District, also called the Tucson Mountain District (TMD). Other than the way in which I was hired, there was another first for me. In the other parks in which I had worked, summer was the season of heavy visitation. Saguaro is just the opposite. Winter is their main season because of the mild climate. Therefore, I was working their off-season.

When this park area was first established, Tucson was a relatively small city (around 40,000, I believe.) Therefore, the two halves of the monument were quite a ways from town. Since then, Tucson has grown so rapidly that it now bucks up against the park on both east and west. The significance of this for me was that I was working city-like law enforcement for the first time, since patrolling the western edge of our district really involved also patrolling the outskirts of the eastern edge of town. A good illustration of this was when ranger Rich Hayes was taking me on an orientation road patrol and noted a house that we regularly passed on duty. He remarked that the owner said that he was going to kill a cop someday. A gunfight had already occurred on the front lawn of the property. Needless to say, Rich had my full attention! I was not able to renew my commission right away, however, since there was no 40-hour refresher course available. For that reason, I had to get my 40 hours piecemeal. Some were acquired at ALETA (Arizona Law Enforcement Training Academy) and the rest from videos, book study, baton training, and firearms qualification.

Married housing is always scarce for seasonal employees, but in this case we had a unique situation. We were given housing at the Madrona Ranger Station near the south boundary of the district. The quarters were a one-story ranch house which we had to ourselves most of the time. To get there involved first entering a controlled area that involved using an access gate, and then proceeding first to the park boundary, and then to the ranger station. The road in was bumpy dirt and sand and seemed hardly maintained. We had some interesting neighbors outside the park boundary. One was Michael Blake who wrote "Dances with Wolves". We never actually saw him, as he had been battling cancer, but his brother paid us a visit astride one of the horses that had been in the movie. Blake had taken such a liking to him that he purchased the animal. Another neighbor was the retired head of ABC Sports, but we never saw him either.

Speaking of horses, one of our responsibilities in order to live there was to take care of the park horses and mules. This involved feeding them and cleaning the corrals and stalls. I was now truly an Arizona ranger! We grew particularly fond of one of the mules named Poncho who was almost as much of a pet as he was a pack animal. He would follow Julie and me around when we were cleaning the corral hoping for a petting or a scratch behind the ears, which we were happy to do.

One other 'perk' was a permanent natural water hole suitable for swimming. This was a welcome relief from the oppressive summer heat. Unlike what many people think, the desert is alive with wildlife. We had a bobcat who regularly visited a water trough right outside the front door and a gila monster which had taken residence under the barn. There was even a report of a mountain lion hanging around, although we didn't actually see it ourselves.

It took 20-30 minutes to get in to the law enforcement office. This only complicated yet another of my most embarrassing Park Service moments. When off-duty, I kept my handgun in a gun locker at the house since we had a child present. One day, after already reaching the office, I realized to my horror that my holster was empty! I had forgotten to retrieve the gun from the gun locker! I headed all of the way back, to the chuckles of my colleagues. One of them later gave me a cardboard cutout in the shape of a gun in case I forgot it again! Amusing as his prank was, I actually used the cutout as a reminder by laying it out where I couldn't miss it in the morning. There is another embarrassing thing that I found in my patrol log. I apparently dropped a set of keys down the toilet, although I do not remember doing so. Nevertheless, since it is in the log, it must be so!

The main road through Saguaro East is the 8-mile long Cactus Forest Drive. It is a paved one-way road that winds through the heart of an extensive saguaro forest. Since it is a lightly-traveled one-way road of a known distance, it is a favorite of local bicyclists. They are required to follow the same rules and regulations as other vehicles, but some of them tend to resist this. For that reason, we spent quite a bit of time dealing with them.

The Sonoran Desert of the southwest is extremely hot and dry in the summer. People have a habit of saying it is 'only a dry heat', but when the temperature slips to 110 degrees F., it is like walking into a sauna bath. The hottest we ever saw it down there was 116 degrees. The hot, dry conditions drain moisture from the human body very quickly. Thus, many of the medical situations that I responded to were heat emergencies resulting from dehydration. I had spent a season at Glacier as a sub-district EMS coordinator, and I more or less served the same unofficial role here. One of my chief tasks was to rehabilitate the first aid cabinet.

As I have already indicated, LE rangers have ballistic vests and some parks are strict, and some not so much, as to when they are to be worn. They aren't exactly the coolest thing to wear in the heat so we balked at wearing them all of the time. We decided that we would be more likely to die of heat stroke than a bullet, so we wore them more or less at our discretion.

While traveling in the air conditioned patrol vehicle, I would wear the vest, but on a foot patrol in the desert - no way! The days of routine 10 mile or more day hikes were over. Three miles in the desert with a pack and defensive equipment was enough to sap my energy.

As mentioned earlier, Tucson was (and I assume still is) bicyclist heaven. We actually dealt with as many or more bicycle violations as automobile ones - everything from stop sign violations to illegal parking. One unusual complaint I hesitate to mention, and will do so as delicately as possible. On 23 July, I investigated a complaint from a female jogger of a suspicious cyclist engaging in 'self-gratification' while riding down a dry wash. I looked for him but, mercifully, found nothing. By the way, later that morning I spent time in the library preparing for a presentation on lightning safety for a staff meeting that afternoon.

Believe it or not, lightning storms can be very severe there. This was related to my EMS duties. Another of my safety duties was the regular inspection of the district fire extinguishers.

Although I was permanently assigned to the Eastside, I was occasionally sent to the Westside to do 'ride alongs'. One of those occurred on 24 July. This turned out to be the second time that I had a weapon out while in the field. The Sonoran Desert has a great variety and abundance of reptile species- some quite colorful. Many pet stores around the country covet them greatly. Therefore, the temptation for poaching them and selling them to these pet shops is also great. There is also a market for rattlesnake flesh and skin. Thus on the 24th, while on road patrol with some west siders, we nabbed some reptile poachers. They gave up peacefully, and we got them on 4 poaching violations as well as a weapons one (They had a loaded .45 semi-automatic handgun). To top it off, the driver had an expired driver's license. One of the poaching violations was for hunting with slingshots. This is not an uncommon way for it to be done. This way the animal can be stunned, then easily caught, while being kept alive for the stores.

I mentioned my handgun. We all had them out and concealed against our thighs as the arrests were in progress since poachers are often armed, and as mentioned above, these folks were.

Another memorable incident while working with the west siders was a first for me. We encountered a vehicle at a turnout one evening containing a gentleman who was contemplating suicide. As I recall, the guy's wife had left him, and he had run a hose from the tail pipe into the passenger compartment for the purpose of asphyxiating himself. Fortunately, we had a lady ranger along who talked him out of it, at least for the time being. It has often been found that women are particularly good at this.

As I mentioned earlier, bicyclists are abundant in the Tucson area, and many of them are not doing it just for social reasons. Many are hard core fitness riders. They don't necessarily like their conditioning runs interrupted by stop signs. We had so many of them on the Cactus Forest loop that stop sign compliance was a constant problem for us, but I found a way to be in two places at once. On the 14th of August, I parked my patrol vehicle in plain view of a busy stop. Then I patrolled in a maintenance vehicle elsewhere. A park employee saw a cyclist surging up to the stop with the apparent idea of blowing through when he saw our LE vehicle. He slammed on his brakes, quivered in brief equilibrium, and then went down in a heap. Since he wasn't hurt, we were able to joke about this later. I was able to make use of the maintenance truck also - I picked up some garbage at the Douglas Springs trailhead!

The next day, 15 August, was my last duty day of the season. I spent it by setting up my decoy stop compliance check again. I also investigated possible cactus poaching. Yes, cactuses are poached both for landscaping and other decorative purposes. I spent part of the afternoon checking for any cattle trespass with Rich Hayes and finished up with the usual final administrative details (weapon cleaning, paperwork, etc.). Then, with another excellent evaluation in hand, I headed home to soggy Illinois with the family. It seemed strange to return to the Mississippi River town of Warsaw - strange because it had been a spring and summer of massive rain and flooding, and we had spent the summer in the dry-parched Sonoran Desert.

Saguaro Scenes

the Madrona Ranger Station

The natural Madrona
water/swimming hole

Saguaro Rangers: Loren Good, Rich Hayes, Spangler

The Madrona residence

Julie Spangler with one of the Saguaro horses.
(photo by Keith Russell)

One of the working mules at
Madrona

SAGUARO - 1994

THE SUMMER OF '94 found me back at Saguaro since I accepted my automatic rehire offer. Once again my law enforcement refresher was taken piecemeal. This time over half was obtained at ALETA and the rest once again with firearms qualification, instructional videos, and independent study. Unlike the previous season, however, I didn't have to wait for the completion of the entire 40 hours in order to receive my commission. The year before I had to complete the entire 40 hours before commissioning since I hadn't been commissioned in 1992. Since I had been commissioned in 1993, in '94 I simply had to complete the hours during the season. This may seem like typical government red tape, but I know from experience that, for once, this government red tape makes sense. When I have come on board in an LE job, after teaching and coaching, it has taken me about 2 weeks to reacquire my law enforcement instincts. The 40-hour refresher helps with that reacquisition.

This summer we were housed in the residential area near the headquarters building. Julie actually volunteered part-time as a receptionist at park HQ. I actually spent about half of the season on a fire security detail in what was called the Reddington Complex Fire. It was actually a series of fires that were popping up all over the area - not just in Saguaro, but also in surrounding national forest and state land. For 6 weeks, I worked the 'graveyard shift' in the area of the Rincon Fire spike camp. This was an assembly area for fire crews, helicopters, and a supply depot for fuel and supplies. It was located at an elementary school and the surrounding school grounds, vacant for the summer. I, and other rangers from the NPS and National Forest Service, provided the security for this spike camp. I will talk about this part of my summer first.

At first, I was working 15-hour days but that was soon changed to 12 hours. My schedule was 2000 hours (8:00 PM) to 0800 (8:00 AM) 7 days a week. In those 6 weeks, I had a total of 1 day off. The good news was that I was picking up a bunch of overtime pay. I had worked late hours before but never all night. The bad news was that I found that I was not designed well to sleep very long in the daytime. I found it very difficult to get a good "night's" sleep. Most of the time, I patrolled alone although my shift was shared by John Bland, who was on special assignment from another park area. We were in separate vehicles, however. The average shift was relatively uneventful with the highlight for me being the food. The firefighters were on a 9000 calorie daily diet, and the school kitchen and cafeteria is where everyone ate. To assure that this diet requirement was met, much extra food was stockpiled. The cooks didn't want anything to spoil or go to waste, so we were encouraged to help ourselves. We had the run of the kitchen to snack at any time. ' It was a dirty job but somebody had to do it!' It was a glutton's dream. There were pies stacked everywhere. Michael Blake even sent some over in gratitude for protecting his home from threatening flames. I was also given full meals to take home to the family after my shift.

There were some incidents, though. One night John Bland called to report shots fired in the area of the spike camp. We arrived to find several people around a table. They appeared to be drunk and had a .32 caliber pistol with which, as I recall, one of them claimed to be shooting at a snake or something. Unfortunately, the firing was occurring in the area where thousands of gallons of aviation fuel were stored to be used by the firefighting aircraft. I shudder to think what would have happened if one of those rounds had penetrated a fuel tank. There were also aircraft parked within pistol range. John arrived first and became the contact officer, and I assumed the role of cover officer. They had tried to hide the gun under the table, but were there more weapons? Bland began a pat down of the individuals - one of the 3 being a woman. She was wearing fairly skimpy and tight-fitting clothing. I had found John to be a very decent and modest man, and he hesitated before frisking her with the comment," I can see that you aren't armed." He didn't so much as touch her. By protocol, he actually should have. She turned out to be the daughter of the school janitor. He later accused John of sexual harassment, on what basis I don't know, because at all times he was the perfect gentleman. Anyway, the dad didn't pursue this and nothing further happened in regards to this incident.

Another incident occurred when I was called to remove a rattlesnake from the lunch room. I had done a biology research project in college involving capturing Prairie Rattlesnakes alive in the Black Hills. The experience proved valuable in removing this Diamondback, which was accomplished successfully.

One incident occurred back at the park while I was on duty at the camp. I received a report of a bomb at the Douglas Springs Trailhead. I headed back there 'running hot' (i.e. with lights and sirens). It was daylight at the time, and I got behind some bicyclists, and they would not move over for my emergency vehicle. This illustrated the arrogance of some of these folks that I periodically encountered. If I hadn't been in a hurry, I would have pulled them over. Nevertheless, I was finally able to get around them, and as I recall, it took about 20 minutes or so to get to the trailhead. We had already notified the Tucson bomb squad, and I got there and found that it was not a false alarm. It turned out to be an unexploded 'Molatov Cocktail' in the brush just off the road and trailhead. (It was a homemade bomb consisting of a bottle filled with an inflammatory and having a makeshift fuse). Fortunately, it was a dud. There was no perpetrator around and the intent was not known. At the very least, had it exploded, it would have started a wildfire in the dry brush to add to an already fire-filled season.

As I mentioned earlier, I didn't sleep well during this time period. As time went on, fatigue began to set in. Although we had a few incidents, such as those I just mentioned, most nights were extremely quiet and, quite frankly, boring. My time alternated between foot patrols, road patrols, and parking patrols. It became more and more difficult staying awake, particularly when parked in the patrol vehicle. During one of those times I had a Forest Service guy as a ride along. Suddenly a red convertible whizzed by me in the parking lot filled with a bunch of loud teenagers shouting insults at us. I immediately headed out in pursuit. Then I felt my partner shaking my shoulder and telling me that I had been dreaming. There was no red vehicle filled with teenagers! The images were so vivid that it seemed more like a fatigue-induced hallucination than a dream. Then there was the morning meal in the dining hall before going off duty. I literally slumped over my meal tray asleep while sitting with Rich Hayes, who was just coming on duty for the day shift. It was just afterwards that he went to a spike camp supervisor and insisted that I receive a day off. I was grateful that he had my back because there was resistance to this at first. He insisted, and the next day I received the previously mentioned lieu day.

So much for fire duty. The rest of the summer was spent doing regular duties at the park. One night I was walking through the brush heading toward the vehicle of possible illegal aliens when I started to step over a large circular dark area. I recognized just in the nick of time that what I was about to straddle was a large coiled rattlesnake! Fortunately, I avoided it in time. You don't spend long roaming around the Sonoran Desert until you realize that everything either bites, stings or scratches. One even has to be careful coming out of the shower because there might be a moisture-seeking bark scorpion lying in the folds of a wet washcloth or on the floor of the bathroom. They are pale-brown, small and with a sting that can occasionally prove fatal. Cactuses, of course, are everywhere. The choia cactus has spines that are particularly nasty. They can penetrate the skin with the slightest touch!

There are Indian pictographs scattered throughout the area, including the park. Unfortunately, like the reptiles, they are prized by poachers. One day I was out on ARPA poaching watch and everything was quiet except for an occasional bunch of javalina working their way through the brush below my elevated perch. Choia segments fall off of the main plants in prickly balls. I looked down at my feet. They seemed to be attracted to my boots like magnets. They were burying their spines deep within the tough leather with the slightest touch. I was ever so grateful that it wasn't my skin!

Paula Rooney was our district ranger and did an excellent job and was great to work for.

One morning, while I was off duty, she came to our residence and requested backup from me. An abandoned vehicle had been found at the edge of our western boundary on an old dirt road. This turned out to be less routine than it first appeared since there was a pile of bloody clothes in front of the car. We searched the area the best we could without disturbing a possible crime scene. Laying on the front seat, I found a wallet with the I.D. of a 17 year old male juvenile. Upon doing a background check, it was found that he had been in trouble with the law a number of times and was thought to be traveling with an even younger girl, whether voluntarily or not it was difficult to know. Footprints led into the desert. We radioed in the situation and waited at the scene, hoping that the two would appear, none the worse for wear. The sun was rising overhead and it was getting hotter and hotter. It was not a good time for a prolonged stay in the desert. Rich Hayes and I followed the footprints and lost them without finding any more sign of the two people. A search was begun by air and more ground reinforcements were brought in. I began searching the residences in the area. In Tucson, some of the folks do everything in reverse. Instead of going south for the winter, they go north for the summer. I came upon just such a residence. There was a fence around the place and after crossing it I noticed a 'Beware of Dogs' sign. I called back to Hayes, who knew the owners, and asked him what kind of dogs. His one word response - "rotweilers!" This was not comforting! This was all complicated by the fact that I had the distraction of an overly eager volunteer searcher with me that I had to look out for. I expected dogs to come leaping out from cover at any moment. Fortunately, that didn't happen, but unfortunately, we did not find these two minors either. I repeat, one of the frustrations with being a seasonal is that you aren't always around to know the rest of the story. At the time I went home for the summer, this incident had not yet been resolved. There was speculation that the young man was laying low until he reached the adult age of 18. Thus his juvenile offenses would be erased. To this day, I have not heard what happened to either of them.

Another situation that I was involved with made nationwide news. One night while I was on road patrol with Rich Hayes, we saw what appeared to be an abandoned vehicle in the Douglas Springs parking lot. At first, it appeared to be the subject of vandalism. Windows were broken and, as I recall, tires were flattened. Upon further investigation, however, we found that this had been the scene of a modern day duel. The story was this: Two guys got into an argument over money in a Tucson residence. They agreed to resolve it in a duel with shotguns at the Douglas Springs lot. They went in separate vehicles, and each even had an individual serving as an attendant (i.e. a second) just like in the old days. When they got to the lot, the rules they had agreed to was, as soon as a foot hit the pavement they could open fire. Fortunately, they proved to be poor shots, although one individual did get hit with a few pellets. The vehicles got the worst of it, although one was apparently able to drive off. The argument began in the Tucson Police Department jurisdiction, preceded through the jurisdiction of the Pima County

Sheriff's Department, and ended on NPS land. Thus there were three agencies involved in the investigation. I was assigned the NPS part. This involved a fist full of paperwork- a part of law enforcement that is all so common but which the public seldom sees.

In reference to this becoming a national story- the next morning the Tucson papers had as a headline," New Gunfight at the O.K. Corral!" Paul Harvey picked up the incident and referred to the 'O.K. Corral' story on his nationally- broadcasted radio show. This didn't sit well with the park superintendent who heard about it first on the news rather than in house.

This was not the most bizarre incident, however. Again, the location was Douglas Springs. Each Sunday morning at approximately 0530 a man would ride into the parking lot on his beat up Kawisaki motorcycle. He would then hike up the trail, and after going about ¼ mile, would strip down totally naked. Then he would go the 9 miles up to Manning Camp and come back and get dressed ¼ mile before the trailhead. (My nickname for the guy was Pervert Pete.) This presented a legal problem for us since the federal magistrate said that we couldn't arrest him. The hang up was that the area in which he was naked was designated wilderness, which meant that there was the presumption of privacy- just like in his bathroom at home! Thus, in his depravity, he had learned how to game the system! This was small consolation to the visitors, especially those with children along, that happened to encounter him along the trail. Finally he actually transgressed in some way. (For the life of me I don't remember what he actually did.) A fellow ranger, Loren Goode, was dispatched to set out on the trail to corral him. Loren actually had to chase down and physically tackle him. With cactuses on both sides of the trail, you can just use your imagination! You just can't make this stuff up!

I can't leave 1994 before mentioning a first for me. One day I was called by ranger Robert Stanton from the west side asking if I would like to earn some overtime on one of my days off. He said that a movie was partly being filmed in his area. The title was "Time Master" and starred Pat Morita of "Karate Kid" fame. He needed an additional ranger for traffic control, control of environmental damage, etc. I was happy to have the overtime and thought that it would be an interesting experience, so I said yes. I expected to be on the periphery of the movie set, mostly directing traffic. This was true only about half of the time, however. Actually, Robert and I took turns, one on traffic duty while the other was on the movie set assuring that environmental disturbances were kept to a minimum. When I was on the set, I mean I was RIGHT on the set. One time, in fact, I was politely asked to move since I was actually in the camera shot. It was a relief how polite and cooperative the movie folks were. The director would say "Ranger Terry, would it be all right if we moved this camera to that spot?" Then I would check to make sure that no plants would be damaged before allowing them to move it. The film crew would wait patiently and without complaint until I approved the location.

This was a revealing experience for me. The filming at our location wasn't to occupy more than a few minutes of movie time, and yet it took all day- and a long one at that. It was a typical summer day in the desert with the sun beating down at well over 100 degrees. This scene involved Morita and two children. They did it over again all day long in the blazing heat. This was hard enough on the kids and the crew and Morita was no spring chicken. I checked to make sure he was not overheating and he seemed to appreciate my concern. The two kids and their mother, who was on the set, were fair-skinned and apparently without sun screen. Therefore, I loaned them mine. Whenever there was a break, the boy would come and ask me how he could become a park ranger. It was touching that he asked how he could be like me. It was kind of like my thoughts at his age.

Anyway, I got a new respect for how hard these people work at their craft. We supervised their cleanup at the end of the day, and they 'policed' up the area well. By the way, we got a nice, catered noon meal out of it, eating with the film folks. As I recall, the film company reimbursed the government for our services. So much for 1994.

The plant that gives the park its name, the saguaro cactus.

Saguaro Sunset

Saguaro Wildlife

Desert Horned Lizard

Bobcat

Gila Monster
- one of only 2 species of poisonous lizards in the world.

1995 - 1996

FOR THE FIRST time since I first started in the NPS in 1979, I missed two seasons in a row. This was because I was deeply involved in the construction of an outdoor running track at Warsaw High School where I was coaching track. This activity occupied both of those summers. Moving along to 1997……

Ozark Natl. Scenic Riverways - 1997

In 1997, I came out of "retirement" to accept a position at Ozark National Scenic Riverways in the southeastern Missouri Ozarks. This was my first time working at a national river. This is a long narrow park area preserving more than 134 miles of clear, spring-fed streams and superb scenery encompassing almost 80,000 acres. It preserves long stretches of the Current and Jacks Fork Rivers. The most popular recreational activities are canoeing, floating, camping, and fishing.

I don't know where to start. Things started badly because I heard that sometime since my last law enforcement assignment a ranger slipped through the cracks before it was found out that he had been a member of some kind of subversive group. The NPS reacted by instituting elaborate background checks for all LE applicants. This was for everyone, NOT just for new applicants. The inevitable bottleneck was the result. This was complicated at Ozark by the fact that the local person through which our paperwork was first filtered was a stickler to ensure that every 't' was crossed and every 'i' dotted. If a section was left blank that obviously didn't apply, he insisted that 'not applicable' (or N/A) was put in. Instead of simply penciling it in himself, he would bounce it back, and the resulting additional delay could be weeks. Until this background investigation was satisfactorily completed, the employee could not be commissioned or recommissioned and could not carry defensive equipment. Since I was the last LEO (law enforcement officer) hired at the park, I was last in line to be checked out.

In spite of this bureaucratic mess, I was assigned to solo patrols in what one permanent ranger called the most dangerous shift in the most dangerous location in the park. He said that I was a target out there and showed his sympathy by slipping me a canister of pepper spray, so that I would at least have that as defensive equipment.

More on that later, but first a little history on the park itself. Local residents around many park areas almost universally appreciate them because of the business and tourism that they attract, as well as the recreational opportunities that are so close by. At Ozark, I found that this was not the case for a lot of the local residents. Some NPS areas were formed from other federal lands and, therefore, were not resented as much by the local folks. Ozark National Scenic Riverways, founded in 1964, encompasses a lot of land that many of the locals have viewed as their own and view this park area as a government land grab. Thus the relationship with rangers was, and is, sometimes strained. I found that this did not make the LE job there any easier. I was to work the whole season in a law enforcement position without a commission and the only defensive equipment the whole time was to be that pepper spray!

Most of the NPS campgrounds that I have encountered have been clean and well managed - not necessarily so at Ozark. As I just mentioned, the relationship between the Park Service and the local folks was sometimes tense. Some of these people had camped, fished, and hunted these areas before the park area was there. Thus I believe that park officials chose to manage them with kid gloves so as not to stir things up. I was stationed at a place called Akers which was along the Current River in the northern part of Ozark. The most notorious campground in my patrol area was called Cedar Grove. During the week it was fairly family friendly- on the weekends, however, not so much. Then there was a lot of drinking, drugs and wild parties not very suitable for family consumption.

This campground drew an interesting cast of characters. We had one gentleman who was so antagonistic toward the government that we were instructed never even to ask for his camping fee and to basically give him a wide berth. Another guy had both hands blown off trying to steal parts off of a power transformer. He was an attentive family man, though. He was training his children how to steal in his place! He would relieve himself in the river, making toilet paper unnecessary! He once ran up to me shouting," Don't shoot ranger - I'm unarmed!".

A more serious incident occurred there one evening just before dark. I was patrolling there, but not with a regular patrol vehicle. Rather, I was in a broken-down maintenance pickup truck. It had no mobile radio and was outfitted with no law enforcement equipment whatsoever. When I climbed in I would have to be careful because there was a big hole in the floorboard. At least if the brakes failed I could put my foot down to the pavement and bring it to a halt! Anyway, I rolled into Cedar Grove at 2100 hours just as an excited camper came running up to report shots fired at the edge of the campground near the river. Some people headed to an outhouse had encountered bullets whizzing over their heads. It was reported that there were 5 men in the shooting party, and they told nearby folks that they were going to "float any responding ranger down the river".

I didn't think that one lonely ranger with only a can of pepper spray presented very good odds. Therefore, I called for backup. Without a mobile radio I tried to get out on my portable. Cedar Grove was a notorious 'dead spot', and I knew I would be fortunate to reach anyone. Thanks to the Lord, however, I was able to reach a couple of other LEOs who responded quickly. As we discussed how to proceed, one of them thrust a shotgun into my hands, and I reminded him that both he and I could get into trouble for this since my background check was not yet back, and therefore I was not authorized to carry a weapon. After a brief pause, he suggested,"If I go down, you take my shotgun!" I agreed and said that I would go in unarmed and could at least dilute any gunfire and serve as an extra pair of eyes. This was particularly important since the suspect campsite was surrounded by thick brush with a lot of potential concealment. The conclusion to this incident was anticlimactic. When these guys saw us they melted into easy submission.

This job provided my first experience with plain clothes undercover work. On one occasion, another ranger and I were assigned to canoe the river in civilian clothes and look for illegal drug activity on the water or on the shore. If we spotted anything we were to report back to uniformed rangers who would then 'reel in' the suspect(s).

On another occasion, my wife Julie had her one and only law enforcement experience. One day, supervisory ranger Bill Terry called and asked if I would like some overtime. I answered in the affirmative. He said that he needed two people posing as a married couple on the river. What better than a real married couple like us. He assured me that the previously used procedure would be used so that there would be no danger of Julie being in harms' way.

Julie and I put the canoe in at Cedar Grove. We hadn't gone more than 50 yards when Bill Terry appeared on the shore, motioning frantically to us to join him. He had corralled 3 escaped felons and wanted me to watch them while he called it in. I placed myself between the suspects and Julie, hoping that they didn't know that I wasn't armed. Julie was actually better armed than me because she had her canoe paddle up and at the ready. I kept my eyes on their hands and, fortunately, everything turned out all right. Nevertheless, I told Julie, that after this, her law enforcement "career" was over!

Another first at Ozark was when, for the first time, I frisked a woman. This occurred late one night when several of us sneaked up on a campsite where suspected drug activity was happening. Remembering the unjust accusations of sexual harassment against John Bland at Saguaro, I was careful to follow the proper protocols for frisking a woman. This involved doing the pat down with the back of my hands. The only other pat down I remember doing that summer involved suspicious characters down from Chicago. The complication here was the baggy clothes which facilitates the hiding of weapons. (We found none, by the way.)

The end of my season was as strange as the whole summer. In this case, on my last day, I ended up on a stakeout with another ranger late at night. I don't even remember why - if I ever knew! Then when I went to the office to process out, no one was there to do my final evaluation or for me to hand in my government property to. Thus I simply left the stuff on my desk and departed. Later, back home, I received a letter containing my evaluation that mysteriously contained my counterfeit signature. The evaluation was O.K. but I didn't take kindly to someone forging my signature! This officially ended a truly strange summer for me.

Alley Mill

Alley Spring

The Spangler Residence

Panorama

WIND CAVE NATL. PARK – 1999

1998 WAS ANOTHER 'summer off' from the NPS for me because we were putting the final touches on our outdoor athletic facility at Warsaw. Nevertheless, in 1999 I was back at it. This time it was another law enforcement position - at Wind Cave National Park in the Black Hills of South Dakota. I looked forward to this because my alma mater, Wheaton College, has a science station in the Black Hills, and as a student I spent 2 summers studying there. An interesting side note to this was that we camped in the Elk Mountain campground while studying in the area. There was a neat little cabin at the entrance to this campground, and I thought at the time that it would be great to spend a summer there. Guess what! That is exactly where my family and I were assigned as living quarters!

Before heading to South Dakota, however, I headed to Lincoln Home National Historic Site in Springfield, Illinois, for my 40-hour law enforcement refresher training. This was convenient, in one sense, being nearby in my home state. In another sense, however, it was not so convenient. This training week occurred on 26-30 April when both my teaching and coaching were still in full swing. Fortunately, the school district allowed me to string together various types of leave days, and an assistant coach took charge of the track team for the week. I was much appreciative of that great cooperation. Rangers from multiple parks were there, and Lincoln Home put on a well-organized training program. Like all of these refreshers the government required a certain number of hours in various subject areas, and allowed some elective hours at the discretion of the training site. After the refresher and the school year were over, it was off to South Dakota.

One other refresher that I was required to do involved renewing my 'red card'. This was my type I firefighting recertification. I originally certified at Glacier and to recertify required a physical fitness test. This recertification involved 8 hours of classroom work in addition to the fitness test, which varied over the years from a step test, to a 1.5 mile fitness run, to the 'pack test' that I had to take at Wind Cave. The dreaded pack test involved carrying a 40-pound pack 3 miles in 45 minutes or less. The catch is that no running is allowed. One foot must be on the ground at all times. Although I made it with plenty of time to spare, it definitely discriminates against short-legged people who may not be able to walk fast enough but are otherwise in fire-fighting shape - just my opinion.

Wind Cave National Park is in the southern part of the Black Hills. The central feature is the cave itself with its famed 'box-work' formations and over 81 miles of known passageways. That is only part of the story, however. The park consists of nearly 30,000 acres of surface area where the rolling prairie of the Great Plains meets the western ponderosa pine forests of the Black Hills. This combination of prairie interspersed with forest creates many inviting habitats for a thriving community of wildlife. Visitors are likely to see prairie dogs, bison, pronghorn antelope, coyotes and, if they are fortunate, even elk, bobcats, or mountain lions. It was in this surface area that I was to spend most of my time.

My first incident of note occurred at 1315 hours on 26 June. I was doing a 'ride-along' with permanent ranger Brad Merrill. As a seasonal ranger, new to the park, I had requested this ride-along in order to become better oriented as to traffic violation procedures in the park. About 5 minutes into this patrol, Ranger Merrill noticed a person that he was acquainted with from nearby Hot Springs. (That was Brad's home town.) This was a lady that had caused problems before. As he approached he found her sitting in the front passenger seat of her car. He immediately observed open containers of beer in the vehicle - a violation. All of this occurred in the parking area in front of the visitor center. I quickly retrieved all of the beer cans, both open and closed, and put them in the trunk of one of our vehicles. Thus, this started off as a simple misdemeanor.

Before I had a chance to completely secure the alcohol, however, the lady became increasingly agitated about things being removed from her car. She began insulting us and shouting loud profanities, mostly directed at Merrill. When he asked her if she had anything else illegal in the car, she said no but said he could search if he wished - again laced with colorful language and sarcasm. When he began to search her purse she became physically violent and began to flail her arms at him, hitting him in the chest. This did no damage since he was wearing his body armor. At that point, he found it necessary to place her under arrest and attempted to handcuff her. She physically resisted and after being cuffed on one wrist, she refused to present the other one and in the process bumped into me. I then grabbed her free arm, and we both wrestled her to the ground. I hammer-locked her arm behind her in order that Brad could complete the cuffing process. While being led to the patrol vehicle, she continued verbal insults, profanity, and physical resistance, including spitting on and kicking Merrill. Brad found it necessary to pepper spray her, and she continued to spit on him and all over the inside of the vehicle.

While this was going on, her husband and their 2 children came out of the visitor center where they had been on a cave tour. I explained to him that it would be much better for her if she cooperated with us. He then tried unsuccessfully to calm her down. Merrill explained to him where we were taking her before we left. As we rolled toward a temporary lockup at the Fall County jail, she continued to be verbally abusive. Brad was driving, and I was sitting in back with the suspect. She was cuffed behind (as we always do), but this didn't stop the spitting. Not only was she spitting on the driver, but she began to "rain" in my direction, also. She took particular interest in my flat hat which I had parked in the back window. She had to put the nasty liquid over her head to reach the hat and sometimes, I confess, I watched with a bit of amusement as it fell short, and she spit on herself! There was nothing amusing about her distracting the driver, however - especially on our winding, hilly road. We had finally had enough. I told her if she didn't stop spitting, I was going to shove her face into the side window so that she couldn't spit on us anymore - better than a traffic accident!

We dropped her off at the jail at approximately 1430 - the whole incident lasting a little over an hour. Merrill and I picked her up again at about 1830 for the transfer to the Pennington County jail for booking. We released her to them at around 2030. That last trip was uneventful since she had morphed into a passive whimpering stage. I couldn't help but reflect on a couple of particularly sad aspects of this situation. First, her family had to witness all of this - so much for a positive parental example! Secondly, if she had only cooperated, this would have resulted in a simple misdemeanor fine. Unfortunately, it regressed into the offense of assaulting federal officers. This could have resulted in a term in a federal penitentiary and thousands of dollars in fines. Fortunately, her lawyer was apparently able to plea the sentence down. Thus I was not called to testify in court. I hope that this whole affair served as a good lesson for her!

Most of the other incidents during this time period were relatively routine - mostly minor traffic violations. My basic philosophy in these situations was to simply give a verbal or written warning unless they were repeat offenders. I have always viewed running stop signs differently, however. My view is: What is hard to understand about the word 'stop'. A citation is in order.

On the 4th of July I had another NPS first. I was sent to Mount Rushmore on special assignment. This is not an unusual occurrence when there is a special event going on in a park, but it was a first for me. Thousands of people show up on Independence Day at Mt. Rushmore since there are special programs and entertainment. At that time the day's festivities concluded with an impressive fireworks display. This was particularly enjoyable since Julie and Michelle were able to come over from Wind Cave for the activities. I was there as part of the reinforcements brought in from various parks to manage the huge crowds. At the pre-event briefing, it was determined that the fireworks would be cancelled if the winds exceeded 15 m.p.h. As the time for them approached, the wind gradually began to increase and reached that magic number. Many people had been waiting for many hours for this light show, so the pressure was on to raise the wind standard, which was done until the program began with winds around 20 m.p.h.

Fireworks at Rushmore are surreal. They spoil you for any other display that you will ever see! Everything bursts above the heads after being set off just behind them. It makes for an incredible and spectacular patriotic experience! I had a front row seat since I was stationed alone on the boardwalk directly under the faces. The only people closer were the ones setting them off. As I said, the winds were up and some of the burning embers were drifting down into the woods around and some of them almost on top of me. Then the finger of ponderosa pines that stretches up toward the faces caught fire, and the estimated 50,000 spectators in and around the park got an additional light show. In fact, several spot fires were started there and the audience had a birds-eye view of Kevin Merrill's Wind Cave fire crew as they hustled up to put them out. By the way, Kevin is Brad's brother.

This fire situation created much anxiety with the administration and those of us involved with security. What if the crowd panicked? This memorial park is located in a rugged area with relatively narrow roads leading in and out. There is a large parking garage which was packed, and people were parked along the road on the back side of the mountain. There was a crude, rough, narrow trail leading down to the latter. I was stationed there to assure an orderly exodus. All at once an ocean of people came out of the darkness toward me. I suddenly knew how Custer must have felt at the Little Big Horn! I managed the crowd as best I could and, as far as I know, no one was injured scrambling down the hill to their cars in the darkness. Fortunately, there was no panic and the Park Service dodged a bullet.

The next incident of note occurred on 17 July. At about 1300 hours I monitored a radio call to Brad Merrill concerning a possible littering incident with excessive drinking at Loop A in Elk Mountain Campground. I notified Brad that I would be responding from the visitor center to that location. As is sometimes the case, this was another occasion that was less routine than it first appeared to be. Merrill arrived a minute or two before me, and we found 4 American Indians at site #3, a man and woman near their vehicle, and another couple asleep up on the hillside. We observed litter all over the place and an open container of beer inside the car. I roused the sleeping folks while Brad did a background check on one of the individuals, which came back positive. There was an active warrant out on him for felony assault. We immediately placed him under arrest. The group claimed that there was a 5th member who was the 'designated driver', but he became angry and took off. We were never able to verify his existence, so we insisted that they wait for us and not drive away because they were intoxicated. Also, none had a valid driver's license. We then transported the suspect to the Fall River County jail.

When we got back to the campsite the other 3 were gone, but the car was still there. Later, it was picked up by person or persons unknown. An interesting footnote to this incident was that it occurred less than 100 yards from our cabin. Julie and Michelle watched the whole arrest from a front window. I later chastised them because if the situation had degenerated into a gunfight, they would have been vulnerable. They were to later 'work' for the NPS in a night research project. All 3 of us helped in this.

It involved a study of the nature of the symbiotic relationship between tiger salamanders and prairie dogs. We surveyed the percentage of prairie dog dens that were occupied by the salamanders. This was the first survey done by Michelle and Julie for the NPS, but I had participated in a one-day Northern Spotted Owl survey back in '91 at Crater Lake.

Saguaro has a variety of species of rattlesnakes, but the Black Hills has only one - the prairie rattler. Nevertheless, it is fairly common there, and the Wind Cave area has its fair share. The night air is cool, and these cold-blooded reptiles have a habit of looking for warm places to hang out, and sometimes this includes the restrooms in Elk Mountain Campground if someone happens to leave the door ajar. On the night of 23 July, I monitored a radio call to Brad Merrill concerning a rattler near the loop A restroom. Brad was farther away than me, so I told him that I would take the call. He had no fondness for snakes in the first place, and when I offered to handle it, he responded, "Please do!" It turned out to be a young one only about 18 inches long. (Full-grown adults usually run about 3 feet.) This one was coiled up just outside the women's side ready to give some sleepy lady on a nocturnal visit the thrill of her life! Various visitors observed from a safe distance as I worked the snake into a garbage bag with a broom handle. I released it unharmed outside the campground.

Although I was officially hired as a Wind Cave ranger, I spent one or two days a week at Jewel Cave National Monument. This small park area had no law enforcement personnel of their own, so Wind Cave 'LEOs' took turns covering that NPS area also. Jewel Cave itself is huge and is known for its calcite crystal formations which gives the cave its name. Unlike Wind Cave, this NPS area has a surface area of only 1,275 acres. It is located only 13 miles west of the town of Custer and about a half-hour drive north of Wind Cave. With such a small area, there is only a mile or so of road distance. There were plenty of speeders, but by the time they could be caught up to, they would be out of my jurisdiction (and I think that many of the local folks probably knew that). This was complicated by the fact that I didn't have radar in my Jeep Cherokee. Thus I spent most of my time on foot while at Jewel.

I patrolled the one trail occasionally but seldom made any visitor contacts there. Most visitors just came for the cave tours. More problems seemed to occur inside Jewel Cave than in Wind Cave. Occasionally, would-be rock hounds would try to collect the crystalline structures, and so I would periodically go under- cover to deal with the problem. I would simply pull a civilian jacket on over my uniform top. It was long enough to cover my 'leather' (defensive equipment) also. I would play tourist and fall in at the end of the line, so that I could observe the whole group. Fortunately, everyone behaved themselves when I happened to be there. I didn't follow in visible uniform for 2 reasons. First, it is unwritten etiquette that we try not to do that because it can distract attention from the interpreter guide. Secondly, on the elevator at the end of the tour, I would casually remove the jacket to reveal the uniform. Hopefully, the word would get around that unsuspected eyes might be watching for any infractions.

An exception to this procedure would be if an interpreter actually called up for law enforcement help. An example of this occurred once when I got a call that some teenagers were refusing to stay with the group and could be in danger of getting lost. In this case, I joined the end of the tour group in full uniform with no comment, just a cold stare at the perpetrators- end of problem!

The summer of '99 was particularly noteworthy for Wind Cave. The area was once one of the locations for the Indian Sun Dance Ceremony. Because it had been outlawed in the country for many years, it had not been held in the Wind Cave area since Crazy Horse had conducted it in the late 1800's. Having been made legal again, the park agreed to allow it here for the first time since the Crazy Horse one. The permit for this ran from 21 July through 5 August. In appreciation for this use of park land, park employees and their families were invited to visit the ceremonies at any time during this period. This was something that normally only American Indians were allowed to attend. In order to go, it was necessary to attend an orientation as to proper behavior and protocol while there. As I recall, there was also a handout to read. At the end of the orientation session, the tribal leader called us to a prayer circle and began praying to his perceived god. This caught me completely off-guard. As a Christian, I could not pray to a false god, so I prayed silently to Jesus instead. Nevertheless, participating in a pagan ceremony continued to bother me for years even though I asked God for forgiveness. Finally, I expressed this guilt in a Sunday school class back home, and I was prayed for in a group prayer. Sometimes expressing oneself to fellow Christians and praying together really helps. It lifted this burden in my case.

I was to acquire a special task for this Sundance Ceremony. Buffalo skulls are part of the ceremony, and one bull had been put down by other rangers after being hit by a car. I was detailed to sever the head and carve the flesh off. I accomplished this, but it was not pleasant. The smell was so bad that it actually made me nauseous, but the Indians got their buffalo skull.

Various park personnel did opt to visit the ceremony, and I was one of them. I drove out to the area in my Jeep Cherokee patrol vehicle, and I left all my weapons in the car as required. No other park people were there at that time. There weren't just Lakota there - in fact, I was shown around by a Seneca tribal member from New York. He showed me all kinds of interesting things about Indian culture, including the construction of teepees that makes them warm in winter and cool in summer. I ate a meal with them and was treated in a friendly and courteous manner. The only exception to this was my own fault. As we were walking around the area, a large man, who looked like a linebacker for the Green Bay Packers, stared grimly and pointed at me. He then pointed at his head and made a long arc with his hand from his head to his waist. I asked my guide what that meant. He told me that I was to remove my hat while in the area - which I did - quickly!

You may notice that I have been using the term 'American Indian' or 'Indian', for short, in my references. As I conversed with my Seneca guide, I was very "politically correct" in using the term 'Native American' to describe these folks. I noticed, however, that he kept saying "Indian" in describing themselves. I asked him which they preferred, and he said that they didn't care, but I was the only one that day that said 'Native American" (More on this in a later chapter.).

I would like to make a few comments about the Sundance Ceremony itself since it is a very dramatic happening. The first thing I noticed was what the bison skulls were for. Young men were moving around dragging the skulls behind them. These skulls were attached to their backs by rawhide thongs connected to pieces of wood imbedded under the skin of their backs. Needless to say, blood and sweat were rolling down their backs. The main part of the ceremony, however, involved imbedding the wood under the skin of their chests and connecting the rawhide to a willow tree which had been cut down and strategically planted in the ground just for this purpose. This would be preceded by a time of purification in a sweat lodge. (We were informed that they would handle any heat related emergencies that resulted, and that ranger EMS would not be required.) A number of the young men would dance around the willow tree until exhausted and would then break free, tearing the rawhide from their chests with results that you can imagine. Like I said, this is a very dramatic and intense affair!

The most traumatic incident of the summer, and one of the most ever for me, also occurred on the surface. The natural entrance to Jewel Cave is located some distance from the visitor center and the main tourist entrance. The historic ranger station is located just above this natural entrance. Daily afternoon tours by candlelight were conducted through this entrance. One day a man harassed a lady tour guide outside of that entrance, an unnerving experience in this out-of-the-way spot. Thereafter an LE ranger was stationed in the area during this tour. When I was on duty there, I normally just sat on the porch at the old station while the tour was going on and until the tour guide was gone. Thus I was in plain view of anyone with any mischief in mind. This would hopefully discourage any 'bad guys'. We call this 'showing the flag'. It was a good time to read the local newspaper.

On 8 August at about 1648 hours, while sitting out there, I received a radio call from the visitor center. I answered but they did not hear me. Then the landline in the cabin rang, and it was again the visitor center reporting that a vehicle accident had occurred on US Route 16 (the one that goes through the monument). The location was reported to be about a mile east of the visitor center. The report also mentioned an injured victim. I requested that KOE 744 (the visitor center) call for the Custer County Ambulance by landline while I called the Custer County dispatch by radio. The VC was on the ball having already called the ambulance. 744 asked me if I wanted EMT interpreter Jill Jaworski on scene. I replied in the affirmative and requested that she bring the cave jump kit and oxygen.

I then proceeded to the scene, running 'hot' (lights and sirens), while calling the Custer County Sheriff's Dept. for backup while enroute. I arrived on scene at about 1659 and observed that there was a single motorcyclist involved. He was lying on the inside of a blind curve and just off of the roadway. I parked just off of the road, on the outside of the curve, with the overhead flashers left on to warn oncoming traffic. Upon approaching the victim, I saw that Jaworski had already arrived and was tending to the victim with the help of a physician who had happened to be passing by. Their patient was bleeding from the head and face, and the face appeared to be badly swollen, especially around the right eye. I identified myself as an EMT and asked if they needed anything from me in that capacity. Jill answered in the negative- that the patient was stable and that they had everything under control, so I put on my LE 'hat' instead.

My immediate critical problem was establishing traffic control. A quick analysis revealed the worst possible situation. With blind curves in both directions along this narrow winding mountain road, safety was a critical concern. What made matters worse was the lack of road shoulders especially where the victim and first aiders were located. They were squeezed up against a rock wall and almost on the roadway itself. Traffic safety had to be dealt with - and fast! Fortunately, a Custer County sheriff's deputy arrived shortly after me. I told him that I would take the eastbound traffic control if he would take the westbound traffic. It was necessary for me to go where I could no longer see the accident scene. Fortunately, three interpreters from Jewel Cave reported to me to offer help. I lined them up at intervals around the outside of the road curve. I would have each oncoming vehicle stop; then I would explain the situation ahead and pass it along to ranger Eric Bissmeyer, a few hundred yards ahead, who had a clear view of the accident scene, and would in turn pass it along to rangers Nancy Bissmeyer and Lori Hamaker. I also used Nancy to pass messages along between EMT Jaworski and myself. Thus I could hoof it back there if she needed EMS assistance from me.

Once the ambulance, wrecker, and other support vehicles had cleared the scene and all accident debris had been cleared from the roadway, I cleared the scene at about 1800. I need to add that only because Jaworski, Hamaker, and the young married couple (the Bissmeyers) were "johnny-on-the-spot" did this very difficult situation end as well as it did. Also, thanks to the Custer County Sherriff's department for their quick response. Finally, thanks to the doctor, whose name I never knew, who defined the meaning of Good Samaritan. As a post script to this incident, I will note that the driver, who was there for the Sturgis Motorcycle Rally, admitted that he was going too fast for the conditions. This was the last incident of note in 1999. There were a couple of other minor traffic accidents but, fortunately, no serious injuries. Once again, back to Illinois at the end of August.

Before moving to the 2000 season, however, I would like to reference a very personal spiritual event that occurred in the latter part of the summer. I had been bitter toward God for the traffic accident that had taken my mother in 1986, thirty-two years after a previous car accident had crippled her for life. Since then my language had become more salty, my temper quicker, my Bible study less frequent, and my prayer life less fervent. Julie and Michelle were planning to head back early for school commitments. As we were sitting down to supper one evening, I began complaining again about my pending decision as to whether to take early retirement from my public school teaching job. This had been going on a while before then, and my griping about public school conditions had become very tedious, and Julie had finally had enough (and justifiably so). She said that she and Michelle might actually go home earlier than planned, so that they didn't have to hear it for a while. I stalked away from the meal and out to the little front porch.

I sat there with only a windbreaker over a t-shirt, and it was a typically cool Black Hills evening. Then it came to me that I needed to learn to trust God again. I prayed and made a simple and seemingly trivial request. I asked God to send Julie out to the porch for a conversation. I vowed to stay out there until she came out. I was shivering, but I remarked to God that he was giving me quite a show. Out to the east there was lightning that lit up the sky. Somewhere out in the darkness to the north a buffalo herd was bellowing in their own unique way, and to the south a coyote was howling. The Lord certainly had my attention! Suddenly the door opened and out came Julie. I remarked to her that my prayer was answered. She asked what I meant. I told her that she was answering a prayer. She said that I was freaking her out since she had come out because there was a distinct knock on the door. I was sitting only a few feet from the door, and no one had knocked! Anyway, we both were then able to enjoy God's show! The Lord does work in mysterious ways! After that my attitude toward Him turned around....a great way to end my tale of 1999!

Wind Cave Wildlife

Badger

A Prairie Rattlesnake

Pronghorn Antelope - the second fastest animal in the world.

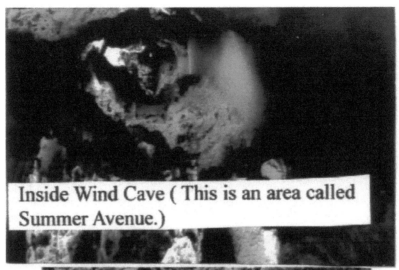

Inside Wind Cave (This is an area called Summer Avenue.)

Wind Cave's unusual 'boxwork'

Panorama

Wind Cave - 2000

I ENTERED THE 2000 season with bittersweet feelings. On the one hand, I was coming back to a satisfying job from which I had received an excellent job evaluation. On the other hand, I knew that there would be no third year. Next year I would be 57 years old - too old for NPS law enforcement. Nevertheless, Julie and I would have the same satisfactory quarters and familiar surroundings. We were 'empty nesters' so it was just the two of us now. I was also now a retired public school teacher, so I was anticipating a much longer summer season. For the first time, I did not have to get back for school, so I was able to work well into the fall. Julie would still head back early to teach.

It was to be another eventful summer. There were quite a number of minor illnesses and injuries to deal with - mostly campground mishaps and bumps and bruises during the cave tours.

We still serviced both Jewel and Wind Cave. Once again both Julie and I participated in the salamander survey and had an additional gig, helping with a pronghorn survey. Once again I was assigned to temporary duty at the Independence Day celebration at Mount Rushmore. This year there was a difference, however.

There was a new seasonal law enforcement ranger at Wind Cave and the ink was still wet on his commission (i.e. He was a rookie). Since I have some critical things to say about him, I will give him an assumed name - John Jones. He was what we called a 'heat seeker' (i.e. one who was always looking for action). Most rangers that I have worked with do not fit into that category, but I ran into one occasionally. Jones was one of those, in spades. I have always felt uneasy working around these thrill seekers. I believe that we should view ideal law enforcement as creating a situation where everything is peaceful and everyone is obeying the law. This, of course, doesn't always occur, but we should always strive for that situation.

I had never really had a situation in the NPS before where I was in constant conflict with another employee, but that was about to change. Jones had been assigned to the 4th at

Rushmore also. At the end of the festivities, thousands of visitors were trying to leave on the narrow mountain road out of there, like a lot of sand passing through a narrow funnel. Jones and I were stationed in the parking garage as people there had to sit and wait their turn to leave. Inevitably, there was a lot of drinking going on. We had been directed by the superintendent in the pre-event briefing to ignore excessive drinking unless the individual(s) was causing trouble. In this case, one group of people was getting pretty well oiled. As mentioned in a previous chapter, my family and I are well acquainted with the implications and potential consequences of drunk driving and I determined to prevent one. Thus I headed over to make contact with them. They were drinking beer out of the back of a pickup as I approached them with a friendly greeting. I asked if they had a designated driver. They pointed to a girl who appeared to be in her upper teens who was a daughter of one of the group. She was sitting off by herself, and as I interviewed her, I observed no alcohol nearby and smelled none near her. She also seemed to be stone-cold sober. I was satisfied. Whether they had planned to have her drive before I contacted them, who knows, but they knew now that they were being watched and that this would now be expected.

When I broke contact with the group, Jones went ballistic on me for denying the opportunity for him to make a bust. He had been standing there waiting for a drunk to get into the driver's seat so that he could make an arrest - so much for preventative law enforcement. What if we had been called away to another situation and a DUI driver had gotten away in the meantime, and what if they had caused an accident that we could have prevented? Guess what! We WERE called away, and the vehicle in question had left by the time we got back. Fortunately, in this case, I assume the sober girl was driving because the folks in question would have assumed that LE eyes were watching from somewhere.

The tension lasted all summer but I will mention only one other incident. One day I was patrolling out on NPS 5 (a dirt/gravel road in the northern part of the park) when I came upon an abandoned car with smashed out windows. As I was checking it out to see if anyone was in trouble or there was any foul play, I received a radio call from Jones requesting my assistance - no emergency indicated. I told him that I had a situation that I was checking out and couldn't help him. I found out later that he threw a fit that I didn't come right away.

Enough of this situation except for one post script. We had a permanent ranger come on board that summer with 20 years of experience who told me that Jones was always telling him how he ought to be doing things. I don't know where John Jones is today, or what he is doing, but I hope he has found out that you can learn more with your mouth closed than with it open.

I already mentioned that I often played tourist in an undercover roll in Jewel Cave, but on the afternoon of 25 July I accompanied a tour in full uniform. I had received a call about a possible problem on a tour in the cave. I arrived partway through it but encountered no problems. In debriefing the tour leader later, I learned that 3 teenage boys had been overheard planning to sneak off of the tour route. In a cave many, many miles long and partly unexplored, this could have proved fatal. By following along behind, I apparently caused them to change their plans.

You can't talk about serving in the Black Hills without talking about the Sturgis Motorcycle Rally which occurs in the first week of August each summer. Sturgis is a small town at the northern edge of the Hills that hosts hundreds of thousands of cyclists at that time. These folks bleed off into all parts of the region during the celebration. This is the strangest collection of bedfellows that you ever saw- everyone from Christian motorcycle clubs to motorcycle gangs. Many, but not all, are fairly well-to-do, including doctors, lawyers, etc. Many are experienced riders, but others are inexperienced 'easy rider' wannabes. This latter group is what we often dealt with as EMS responders.

One such incident occurred on the pigtail curve on highway 87 which is so sharp that it actually passes under itself. The motor- cyclist was distracted by wildlife along the road and failed to make the curve. He suffered what appeared to be a severe head injury and although he was conscious enough to talk, required immediate transfer to the hospital in Custer. This was one of those frustrating ones for which we never heard the diagnosis or final outcome - at least not that I can remember.

In another incident there was no doubt as to the outcome. Fellow ranger Glen Yanagi and I were doing our fire qualification 'pack test' for the 2000 season. Thus we were in our work-out clothing when we received a radio call that a serious motorcycle accident had occurred on Highway 385 near the junction of route 87. Without changing clothes, we hurried to the scene and found chief ranger Denny Zieman already there. The situation involved a husband and wife riding double. They had planned to turn off on 87, but the man realized he had missed the turnoff and hit the brake. He was not hurt, but she was thrown violently over the front and suffered massive head trauma. Her arms were posturing, indicating severe and ultimately fatal brain damage. There was nothing we could do except direct traffic until the body could be removed. This is always a sobering experience which one never gets used to. The bottom line is that I have never responded to a traffic accident in the Black Hills while on duty that didn't involve a motorcycle. (Once I did help out at a two-car accident outside the park while off duty.)

The Lookout Point Trail Loop begins off of route 87 and ends up at the same point a little less than 5 miles later. Several other trails branch off of it, however. Late in the summer a lady became lost on it. Fortunately, she was located by means of her cell phone signal. She complained that the trail was not well marked. I was detailed to find out if her complaint was well founded. I was to take to that trail and pretend that I knew nothing about being in the woods - no compass, map, or anything (just like some visitors!). I found that, indeed, if someone inexperienced took this trail, they could become confused. Thus the next day, I headed out with trail markers to remark it. They were quite cumbersome as I rattled along with them. I had dropped down into the Beaver Creek drainage where the vegetation was thick and shoulder high on both sides of the trail. All of a sudden 4 heads popped up about 200 yards ahead. They turned out to be 2 cow bison and their 2 mostly grown calves.

The rattling of the plastic trail markers seemed to disturb them. They immediately headed toward me on the run. I dropped the markers but kept my day pack on as I headed toward a foothill in the opposite direction. As I turned around periodically, I could see that they were closing the distance rapidly - 150 yards, then 100. I had my 9mm handgun with 14 rounds in and 2 extra 13-round magazines in my ammo pouch, and even though they weren't bulls, I didn't like my chances with this. I decided to try and break up the charge by heading up the slope of the hill. Hopefully, this would discourage them. As I was running, I couldn't help but have an amused thought. My tombstone would say: 'trampled to death by buffalo', just like for an old westerner caught in a stampede! As I huffed and puffed up hill, and they were 50 or so yards away, I noticed some deadfall timber down a gully to my left. I headed down there to discourage them from running through all of this rough stuff. When I did this, however, I was out of their sight in the trees, and they ran right past me. I doubled back behind them and went back to the trail and headed home.

When I got back, the biology research staff was incredulous that these cows would have done this - buffalo bulls yes, cows no. The theory was put forth that they were headed back to the herd, and I just happened to be in the way. I can't say, but all I know is that they just kept coming and straight at me...fast! I went back the next day and finished up the trail marking, but this time with a shotgun. There was not a bison in sight this time. It was also necessary to change the trail map available to visitors- as it was wrong in one place.

The next year, while attending my class reunion at Wheaton College, we discussed notable events that we had experienced. I related this incident to them. One lady asked me how I could think rationally at a time like that. I answered that when you are involved in enough emergency situations, you kind of get used to it. I should have mentioned that there was another more important reason. In that situation and many others, I just have had the feeling that God has things under control and that things are happening the way that they are supposed to. This is always calming and comforting.

The cave itself is the chief drawing card in the park but the wildlife viewing isn't far behind - especially the buffalo (bison). They are fascinating to watch. As you watch a herd, it is interesting to note how they move. Even when they don't seem to be moving at all, in what seems to be no time at all, the entire herd has vanished. They pay no attention to road traffic, and I would sometimes spend most of the day dealing with buffalo 'road jams' as they would move slowly across the road or hardly move at all.

They were moving fast one time that I recall, however. We had 'buffalo on roadway' signs that we would put up when they were on the road near one of our many curves to warn drivers of the furry roadblock ahead. Sometimes I would have the frustration of completing the sign posting just in time for one of those magical moves to leave or to block the road somewhere else. They just had no interest in cooperating with me! In one particular case, a herd was on the road at Buffalo Flats right where it opens up out of a narrow gorge on route 87. As I walked out to put up the sign, the whole herd suddenly stampeded towards me. They weren't charging me this time, but I was definitely in their way and there was little room in the narrow gap on either side of the road for both them and me. Charging or not, I didn't fancy being trampled in a buffalo stampede, and there was a virtual wall of them headed my way, so I beat a hasty retreat to the patrol car and quickly did a U-turn and headed out of Dodge! I was glad that there weren't any visitors around because they surely would have gotten a chuckle out of seeing a ranger running for his life while lugging a road sign!

On 24 August a monumental occurrence was to descend on the Black Hills, the Jasper Cave fire, which was to become the largest wildfire in South Dakota history. It was reported at 1417 hours that afternoon and would eventually consume tens of thousands of acres. The name comes from the fact that it started in the area of Jewel Cave National Monument known as Jasper Cave. An investigation revealed that a mentally ill woman apparently started it. I had patrolled in the area only the day before.

I never actually acquired a role on this fire. I had a distressing call from home just after I was detailed to help provide security on the fire. My wife Julie had gone back for her junior high English teaching job, and she was on the phone. She stated," I don't want to worry you, but I am on a heart monitor right now." To say I was worried is an understatement. I felt so helpless from 900 miles away! I quickly contacted Denny Ziemann, and he graciously excused me from the fire assignment so that I could deal with this family emergency. I contacted our family doctor back home to discuss the situation. Should I head home immediately? He said to sit tight and didn't seem overly concerned. It turned out that the irregular heartbeat was the result of excessive caffeine - something that women are apparently particularly susceptible to. What a relief when the doctor said that it was temporary and not serious! After this scare, however, Julie and I decided - no more 6-week separations!

Although I ended up without a roll in this fire, I was involved in 2 others, both within the boundaries of Wind Cave. One was a fairly substantial one in the northern part of the park. Although I was red-carded, I wasn't assigned to the fire line. I simply carried supplies back and forth to those who were. The only other duty that I had was to walk the edge of the extinguished burn area looking for another bison skull for the Sundance ceremony. A curious aspect of this was that the fire hadn't been reported as fully contained yet. This illustrates how very conservative these reports tend to be. Although I saw no flames or even smoke - better safe than sorry!

The other fire I refer to occurred at the extreme south end of the park and was only an acre or less in size. It occurred during a severe lightning storm, and I believe that I recall seeing the actual strike that caused it. At any rate, I headed out there to check it out and was the first park person on the scene, although some local folks from just outside the boundary were already there. A fire crew plane, already in the air, apparently for fires elsewhere, dropped slurry (fire retardant) and put it out almost as quickly as it started. I walked through the slurry-laden grass while stamping out the remaining hotspots. Slurry, by the way, looks and feels much like liquid laundry detergent but doesn't do much for the spit shine on your boots! Fires are often named for places or people, and they were going to name this little one after me - but then didn't. So much for my claim to fame!

So much for an eventful 2000 season and what I expected to be my last as a law enforcement ranger.

More Wind Cave Wildlife

Prairie dog

Bison

Part of the Wind Cave herd - one of the few genetically pure ones left in the world.

The Spangler residence at Wind Cave

'Target Room', inside Jewel Cave

The restored historic ranger station

Formations that gave Jewel Cave its name.

Calcite crystals

Frostwork

Spangler's 'leather'

Herbert Hoover Natl. Historic Site/Glacier N.P. - 2001

2001 WAS TO be another season of firsts for me. As a teacher retiree, I was now able to work the full 6-month summer season and did so - but not at only one park, but two. I started out in the spring at Herbert Hoover National Historic Site. This preserves President Hoover's boyhood home and surrounding buildings. It lies adjacent to the Herbert Hoover Presidential Library - both within the city limits of West Branch, Iowa. The library is not technically part of the NPS area. The historic site itself consists of almost 187 acres. About 75 of these acres consists of a restored tall grass prairie. The rest of the grounds consist of the birthplace cottage, the blacksmith shop, the one-room schoolhouse, the Friends meeting house, (Hoover was a Quaker), and the burial site of Hoover and his wife. There are also other historical residences on the grounds.

With law enforcement no longer available to me, I was hired in an interpretive position. This was night and day different from the law enforcement and general ranger positions that I had mostly been doing, and was the first interpretive position I had held since Isle Royale in 1985. In those jobs, I of course, had regularly assigned hours but was usually on my own in determining the activities that I would do during those hours. Not so in this job. There was a very regimented schedule. This was very much like school teaching in that each minute was accounted for. Each member of the interpretive staff would alternate between manning the visitor center desk and leading tours of the above mentioned facilities. These tours had to start precisely on time, last 30 minutes, and move precisely so that the next tour didn't catch up. Then it was back to visitor center duty. School groups occasionally requested tours of the prairie, which I much preferred, but these were few and far between.

Although this job was mundane and boring, it did have advantages. This was the closest to my permanent home that I had ever worked. It was only a couple of hours away and allowed me to commute back there on my weekends. The regular daytime work hours also helped with this commute. The irony was that I actually had piles of living space since I was bunking in one of the large historical houses. Thus Julie joined me there occasionally for a week's stay. Unlike most parks, the spring and fall are the big tour times because this park area caterers to school groups.

With the slower summer season at hand, I was able to work out a deal with the Park Service to go back to my beloved Glacier for the summer season and then back to Herbert Hoover for the fall. Thus, with a short break, Julie and I headed west. We got there just in time for orientation. The last leg of our journey was around a winding road through the foothills of the Blackfoot reservation during a snowstorm (yes, in June!) Although I was now to work an interpretation position there, the first orientation topic was on bears. (In Glacier all employees are required to have some bear training.) This was a more pleasant gig, not only because of the location, but also because of the variety of tasks and the less intense timetables than at Herbert Hoover. This was my first time working on the west side of the park, and part of my time was working the Apgar visitor center. I also conducted 2 different nature hikes, one of half-a-day and another of shorter length. In addition, I conducted boat tours on Lake McDonald and presented a slide program entitled "Predators of Glacier National Park," both in Lake McDonald Lodge and in a campground.

Waterton Lakes National Park, Canada, is adjacent to Glacier's northern boundary and the two parks together form Waterton-Glacier International Peace Park. I participated in a liaison with Canadian personnel at a Canadian visitor center in West Glacier celebrating this unique relationship. This was a rewarding experience since it was the first time that I had ever worked with Canadians.

Another great thing about this job was that Julie got to see Glacier for the first time. When we first drove the Going-to-the-Sun Road, Julie's comment was," I don't know how to describe this!" Another time at Sun Point, she said that she didn't know where to point the camera first. We had an apartment in the West Glacier housing area which was small but adequate. She had to go back early for school, but the train stop was within walking distance of our residence, and it was a straight shot to Chicago (although a long one!).

There is a neat private organization called ' A Christian Ministry in the National Parks' which is active in some of the larger parks, including Glacier. This is a program in which young ministerial students get a chance to practice giving sermons and other church responsibilities while giving church-goers Sunday services while away from home. These young folks acquire jobs during the work week for the summer, either inside or outside the park. We had attended these services while working at Crater Lake, but here we participated on a support committee for this Glacier group which we found to be a worthwhile task. We were able to give support on Sunday by attending their services and helping in any other way needed. This was possible because I requested that one of my days off would be Sunday, and the request was granted.

Although I was glad to be back at Glacier, one of the things that bothered me was that everything seemed to be compartmentalized. An example of this occurred when I was working the information desk at the Logan Pass visitor center. This occurred on a regular basis and was normally decent duty. On one particular day however, an incident occurred that left me very frustrated. I didn't find out about it until it was over. A person had a serious medical issue on the Hidden Lake Trail only about 100 yards from the visitor center. Instead of advising EMT Spangler in the VC, law enforcement was called from well down the Sun Road. I had a medical kit right there. I had already received a Special Achievement Award from the park in 1987 as an EMS coordinator, but, as is often typical with the government, the powers that be couldn't think outside the box. Since my job description that summer didn't include EMS, it apparently didn't occur to anyone that I could have reached the victim and given aid in a matter of seconds. I never did learn of the patient's outcome.

The other problem that stands out that summer was a more chronic one. It involved the video equipment for my slide program. We did not yet have a Power Point system and were still using a dual slide projection system with regular slides. A rule of thumb is that the slides should follow and support the speaker. The speaker should not support the slides. In other words, one slide should flow into another and not be compartmentalized. Saying things like: "This is a picture of…."; "This slide shows….."; "Isn't this a nice view of…." is a sure cure for insomnia! A smooth narrative simply enhanced by the pictures is much more palatable to most folks. This is only possible, however, when the presenter and the slide order are coordinated. This was not always the case with our equipment, unfortunately. For reasons unknown to me to this day, the slides would sometimes appear in a random order that didn't match my presentation. During those times I would have no idea what was going to pop up next. To say that I had to adlib is an understatement! I would come clean with the audience and turn it into sort of a comedy routine when this happened. To compound the problem at the lodge, the remote control I used was not reliable and the projectors were set up in the balcony at the opposite end of the room. Therefore I recruited Julie to go into the balcony and manually advance the slides when I gave her the signal by ringing a bear bell. As fate would have it, the NPS regional director for interpretation happened to be visiting Glacier during this particular time and was at my program. He came up afterward and told me that he sympathized with my situation and appreciated my innovation. This was a gratifying end to an otherwise frustrating evening.

Despite all of this, it was great to be back in Glacier once again. The scenery and wildlife alone made it all worthwhile. Speaking of wildlife, Julie and I experienced interesting incidents a couple of times as we made the short walk from our residence to Apgar Village. One day, while strolling along that connecting pathway, a young black bear poked his head up above some waist-high vegetation near the trail and watched us go by. Julie thought it was cute and nicknamed the little critter 'Teddy'. In the same area, on a later day, what was probably the same bear romped along beside us briefly, and we saw that it wasn't so small after all. Although the animal was not aggressive at all, Julie no longer found 'Teddy' so cute!

Julie headed back on the Amtrak to teach school in mid-August and I drove back in September. I was to have a short time at home before heading back to Herbert Hoover for the fall.

As previously mentioned, unlike many parks, the spring and fall are heavy visitation times for Herbert Hoover because it caters to school field trips. I believe that this is a good thing since schools spend little enough time these days on teaching American history. The only downside of this is that some teachers don't control their students that well. This bothered me particularly at this NPS site since, in my opinion, the antiques and relics in the buildings, particularly in the birthplace cottage, are not that well protected. At the time I came there, they had experienced irreplaceable books being stolen.

I can't move on to 2002 without noting where I was when 9-11 occurred. When the attacks happened, I was at home between the Glacier and Herbert Hoover assignments. I watched in horror on Fox News. Later that week, I was back working in Iowa and didn't have full TV service in my quarters, so I picked up news reports across the street at the local Laundromat.

Backcountry Dwellings - GNP:

Granite Park Chalet

The Swiftcurrent Lookout

Slide Lake Trail Cabin

Indian Paintbrush

- a common sight in Glacier.

HERBERT HOOVER - 2002

IN 2002 IT was more of the same at Herbert Hoover except that I participated in a prescribed burn on the tall grass prairie. This is necessary periodically in order to prevent other vegetation from invading the prairie (i.e. succession). In order to participate, it was necessary for me to renew my firefighting 'red card' certification. After successfully recertifying, I ended up manning a red line hose to aid in controlling the burn. The fire hadn't been lit up for long before increasing winds caused us to abort the whole thing, so we used our hoses to put the fire out. The prairie lies adjacent to the I-80 interstate, and the smoke was blowing across that road. Thus the decision to abort was a good one. I was almost overcome by the smoke as well.

Sometime between my duty in 2001 and 2002 the age restriction for LE seasonals was dropped. I heard that this was the result of an age discrimination lawsuit by someone, but I have no firsthand knowledge of this. Nevertheless, it was decided at Herbert Hoover to add a seasonal LE, and I was offered and accepted the position. This required me to have another 40-hour refresher, and the one that was still available was at Yellowstone. Thus in early June, Julie and I headed west. This turned out to be partially work and partially vacation. When class ended at 1700, I would pick up Julie at the motel just north of the park in Gardiner, Montana, and we would sightsee in the park with plenty of daylight left in those long June days. Other than the regular required subjects, there was an emphasis on Islamic terrorism since 9-11 had so recently occurred.

Upon returning home, my commissioning was delayed well into the fall because my background check was delayed. Thus I took up my interp. position once again until it was completed. When my clearance came through, the Herbert Hoover superintendent decided not to fill the position after all. Thus, all of the government expenses - meals, motels, and other travel expenses, paid for by the taxpayers, were totally wasted! I had received a call from the regional law enforcement director that I was good to go, so I was all dressed for the party but nowhere to go! This is your government in action, folks!

A much more serious issue was going on at this time, however. My dad's health was going downhill and I was called to the nursing home more frequently now for various medical emergencies - one hour and 55 minutes to the nursing home from work. I finally had to use my emergency leave and was not able to return to work before the season was over. We lost my dad that fall, and this brought an extremely sad end to my 2002 season.

Herbert Hoover Birthplace

The tallgrass prairie

The rural schoolhouse

The Quaker Meeting House

The blacksmith shop

Tonto National Monument - 2003

THE 2003 SEASON brought yet more new experiences. Julie and I were headed north to teach in a Christian school system for the first time in the fall, so I was looking for a short season. Such an opportunity presented itself at a park area that I had never heard of before I applied for a law enforcement position there - Tonto National Monument. A permanent LE had left, and they did not yet have a new one on board. I was to fill the gap for 6 weeks or so. One bit of good news with this was that we also inherited the permanent ranger's residence, so we had plenty of room in a nice ranch house, although some other workers used part of it periodically.

Tonto National Monument is a small park area encompassing only 1,120 acres. It was established in 1907 to preserve 3 cliff dwellings of the Salado Indians. It is located in the Arizona desert about 2 ½ driving hours east of Phoenix. This is a remote area except for a nearby Forest Service campground and the small towns of Roosevelt and Globe.

This was my first position involving proprietary jurisdiction. I will explain. Law enforcement in this country is limited by authority and/or jurisdiction. Authority is the scope of the violations that can be enforced. Jurisdiction is the geographical area that these violations can be enforced in. This assures that in our republic no individual law enforcement agency can become too powerful. In the NPS, each park with a law enforcement division has one of 3 types of responsibility. The larger parks (e.g. Yellowstone and Glacier) usually have exclusive jurisdiction. This means that no other LE agencies have enforcement authority within the park. In concurrent jurisdiction, Park Service LE rangers and LE officers in the area surrounding the park have equal enforcement authority within the park area (e.g. Wind Cave and Saguaro). With proprietary jurisdiction, the LE agencies outside the park have the primary enforcement responsibility, with park personnel acting in more of a support role. This is usually the case with very small park areas and a small law enforcement presence (e.g. Tonto and Lincoln Home). The trend is toward concurrent jurisdiction because this gives those parks built-in LE reinforcement.

This area receives very few visitors and is closed at night since there is no in-park campground. Thus I had regular daytime hours. We had no patrol vehicle - only a regular park utility pickup. It had no radio which really didn't matter since my hand radio could reach the visitor center, and we had no dispatcher anyway. Mostly, I just patrolled the limited trail system on foot and occasionally covered for an interpreter in the visitor center. I also hung out occasionally in the cliff dwellings and conversed with the occasional visitor. Therefore, I was mostly on my own. If the truth be known, there was very little for me to do.

I am getting ahead of myself, however. Before the above duties, it was necessary for me to renew my LE commission. Before showing up at the park, I picked up 16 hours at Indiana Dunes National Lakeshore which is located just east of Gary, Indiana. More hours were obtained with self-study at Tonto, and firearms qualification was completed at nearby, and equally obscure, Montezuma Castle National Monument.

As I said, most of my short season at Tonto was very routine and 14 June definitely started that way. It was not to remain so, however. At shortly after 0730 while opening the park with fellow employee Janet Lenon, I noticed significant litter just outside the locked entrance gate. This litter consisted of a folding stool, a small shag rug, some unopened beer cans, and a coffee can containing unknown residue. Three leaking cans of beer had apparently been dropped. Also found was a brown leather coin purse with an empty lipstick case inside. At first, Ranger Eddie Colyott and I treated this as a simple littering incident, possibly some kind of drunken activity, since it had occurred on a Saturday night. It was puzzling though, since some of the beer cans found had not been opened - not typical after a drinking party. I called the local sheriff's department and medical facility to find out if they had any incident-related contacts during the night. There had been none. I threw away the expendable items, and I wrote a lost and found report for the rest. This was unfortunate since the chain of evidence had been compromised for what was to look more and more like a serious crime in the days ahead. At this time, however, the incident was still being treated as routine, so I took my regular 2 days off on the 15th and 16th.

Upon returning to duty on the 17th, I was immediately informed by Acting Superintendent Keith Payne that an abandoned vehicle had been discovered by maintenance workers the previous day in the leech field near the employee housing area. It was a pickup camper. Very ominously, the camper door and both cab doors were open and the keys were in the ignition. Personal belongings were scattered all around. Also ominously, no recent activity had occurred on the owner's credit card or bank account. The Gila County Sheriff's Department was called, and they came and verified that the vehicle belonged to a woman named Jane Doe (real name withheld here). She was apparently missing since further investigation revealed that her pickup truck had been at that location since at least the early morning of the 14th. A park employee out walking his dog at 0630 that morning saw the truck at that location and thought he saw someone walking around it 30 minutes later. He also heard doors closing around the same location. An investigation revealed that no one could be found who had seen the woman since 6 June. We now considered the possibility that this might be connected to the "littering" incident. Therefore, I contacted our maintenance personnel and had them, with gloves on, recover as much of the discarded litter as they could find (all but one beer can). There had been beer cans found with the pickup, also. I then called the county investigator about the possible connection between the 2 incidents. Since the same brand of beer cans had been found at both sites, we checked the lot numbers from the cans at both locations and found that they matched, linking the 2 incidents. The county investigator picked up the collected evidence from us and search plans for the lady were initiated, including a helicopter search.

From the beginning of the investigative process, I acquired witness statements from all NPS employees and their associates who had any knowledge of the incident. As mentioned earlier, the Monument had only proprietary jurisdiction, so the county people were in charge of the show. Nevertheless, I kept in constant communication with them. We conducted a foot search of the leech field area with negative results. We enlisted Ranger Colyott's help in searching for her since he knew the monument area better than the rest of us. We searched through the 18th in the monument and then, to my surprise and dismay, the search by local police was called off. Ranger Colyott and I then participated in a search of U.S. Forest Service campgrounds. Then word was received of a possible sighting on 15 June at an area store of a woman matching Jane's description. At this point official participation in the search by NPS personnel was ended.

Word began to circulate that Jane was an active drug user in the Phoenix area. Thus, it began to be speculated that this was a body drop because she had somehow offended some entity in that culture. She was also a middle-aged, overweight woman who was handicapped (crippled).

Around that same time an attractive young woman went missing elsewhere in the country. The search for her went on for weeks - as it well should have. I couldn't help but notice the disparity, however. If Jane had matched that description, would she have received more attention? I honestly don't know, but I decided to do some unofficial looking on my own.

I roamed around the monument on foot while looking for vultures overhead and using my nose to search for the smell of death. I crawled into road culverts while covering my hands to avoid being burned on the metal that was heated by the desert sun. The results of all this - nothing. I finally had to give up. As far as I know, she was never found - at least not that I have heard.

On that sad note, I will end this chapter on Tonto. In mid-July Julie and I headed back home to pack up and head to northern Illinois to teach at a Christian school there.

The Spangler quarters

Panorama

The Lower Ruins

The Upper Ruins

Ruins interior

WHITE SANDS NATL. MONUMENT - 2004

THE SUMMER OF 2004 found me at White Sands National Monument, again in law enforcement. This New Mexico park area comprises 145,000 acres. Located in the south-central part of the state, it is bordered on the north and south by the White Sands Missile Range, on the west by the San Andres Mountains, and on the east by Holloman Air Force Base. As the name implies, it was established to preserve the dunes of the glistening white gypsum sand dunes of the Tularosa Basin. The nearest town is Alamogordo, about 15 miles away. For lodging, Julie and I were assigned a mobile home - our first experience with one of these. It was not great, but tolerable.

Once again it was necessary to complete a 40-hour law enforcement refresher, but since I had worked law enforcement the previous summer, I did not need to complete the hours before recommissioning. Therefore, I was able to pick up the hours during the course of the summer. The bulk of those hours were picked up with an 8-hour course in Alamogordo (search & handcuffing techniques plus defensive tactics) run by the city police dept. and 20 hours at Big Bend National Park, just north of the Mexican border in Texas. There was a big emphasis there on border security, and there was a mix of NPS & Border Patrol agents in attendance. It was there that I learned firsthand about all of the problems along the border. It also pointed out the conflict within the Park Service law enforcement community between personnel who consider themselves cops first and rangers second and those who view themselves the other way around. I have always considered myself in the latter group, which might also be called the 'old-time' rangers. The trend seems to be toward hiring people who are cops first and who do not need to have as strong a conservation/preservation ethic as was the case before. I believe that this trend has been stimulated by the terrorist attacks on 9-11. One other thing that was new to me was that my annual background check did not come back approved until 13 August. Before this season, I had to have that background/security check done before re-commissioning. The holdup was apparently due to the fact that I had neglected to tell the government of my location during August and September of 2003. (We were in temporary housing before moving into permanent ones as we began our new teaching jobs.) Anyway, back to White Sands.

My first full day of commissioning, after the background check and all the other red tape was completed, was Friday, 2 July. It was also a full moon night and my first night on solo patrol. In spite of the sensitive security areas all around, or perhaps because of it, this was an area of extremely low incident of anything faintly resembling crime. (There were, after all, armed military MPs all over the air base and missile range around us.) I still was not comfortably familiar with the area, and one sand dune there looks pretty much like another. Because of that, my first controversial incident happened that first solo night patrol.

Unlike most parks, a lot of the visitation occurs in the evening and at night since daytime temperatures regularly reach well above 100 degrees in the summertime. The visitation is especially high on full moon nights when the park presents special programs, and local folks come for late picnics and recreation after the desert cools down. My first solo patrol was one of those nights. As I drove around the road loops, mindful that fireworks are prohibited in the park, it was also necessary to look out for beach balls bouncing into the road and frolicking children chasing them. There were people everywhere, and looking out for traffic was sometimes the last thing on their minds. At about 2130 hours, I received a radio call for backup from one of our lady LE rangers in regard to a drunk woman in the dunes. A local sheriff's deputy had already responded, but I tried in vain to find the location. The next day, she reported the incident to our supervisor and accused me of being a coward and being afraid to respond- of all things. I was outraged and told my immediate supervisors that, and what actually happened. They apparently accepted the truth based on the performance rating that I received at the end of the season. Nevertheless, I should have received an apology from the lady, but it didn't happen. I never did trust her after that.

Most of the summer, except for full moon nights, was mostly quiet with a low-level number of law enforcement incidents. As I said, the reason for this is probably at least partly because the area bristles with security enforcement from us, the border patrol, and the Air Force military police. My average day was usually very routine, consisting of building security checks, road patrols, foot patrols, the inevitable paperwork, and giving an occasional verbal or written warning for minor violations (usually traffic or parking ones).

One surprising thing, considering the often oppressive heat, was the lack of serious EMS calls. Most of these incidents were heat-related, but not as many as I would have expected. One victim was taken to the hospital by ambulance, however. The fact that there are relatively few backcountry hikers/campers and no auto campground certainly contribute to there being minimum problems in this area. Picnicking is the most popular, and relatively safe, activity.

As I mentioned, on the law enforcement front, everything was low volume and low key.

I didn't issue a citation until one day at the end of the season. Most violations were relatively minor and often out of ignorance, so a little education rather than punishment was all that was needed. The exceptions were for a couple of illegal backcountry campsites in ecologically sensitive areas. Legal camping areas were well explained and marked, and there was really no excuse. One involved a group of 9 college-aged people who were not happy when I wrote them up until I explained that I could legally fine each one $50, but if they had a good attitude about it, I would only give the group a single $50 dollar one for the whole group. They decided to have a good attitude. It is always good to leave people feeling that you are more of a friend than an enemy, if possible, since another cop someday may need them as witnesses for more serious incidents. After all, we are all in this citizenship thing together. In the other illegal camping situation that day, a good attitude was not forthcoming. This involved a man and his female companion. He insisted on posturing for his female friend - not an uncommon occurrence in these situations. He played the indignant macho role, but his bankroll became $50 less, regardless. I actually issued my only 4 citations of the summer that day, and it only occurred because I was looking in the backcountry for a missing visitor.

An embarrassing incident also occurred that summer. One day there was an antique car show in the area. I noticed a 50's era car going by the visitor center. Since it was a convertible, it was easy to notice that no one was wearing a seat belt. I immediately pulled them over and was told that seat belts were not required in antique cars. I hadn't heard of this and thought that the occupants may have been feeding me a line. I called in and found that they were right, and I was wrong. I apologized with egg on my face!

My season ended with a more serious incident. On my last full day of duty, an illegal alien blew through the nearby Border Patrol station and ran into a ditch only a couple of hundred yards from our housing area. He then ran off into the desert. In coordination with the Border Patrol agents, I notified our various residents and recommended that they lock their doors. Then I headed out into the park in search of the individual. I had negative results. One doesn't last long out there without food and water, so the desire to return to civilization would be great, and he wouldn't have to go far in most any direction there without running into a gun-toting official of some kind. Nevertheless, this had not yet occurred before Julie and I had packed up and headed back to Illinois.

White Sands

Panorama

White Sands Headquarters

Hedgehog Cactus

EFFIGY MOUNDS NATL. MONUMENT - 2005

IN THE SUMMER of 2005, Julie and I decided to overcome the ever present problem of finding Park Service married housing by finding a job close to home. That way she could stay home, and I could possibly commute back and forth, at least intermittently. Alas, there were no law enforcement jobs close by. However, an interpretation position popped up at Effigy Mounds National Monument, and I was headed off to Iowa. Not only was this just a 4 hour drive back home but, since it was a part-time job (32 hours per week), I was on for 4 days and off for 3. This made a weekly trip home highly manageable. Although the park itself had no housing, I was able to find a satisfactory apartment just across the Mississippi River in Prairie du Chein, Wisconsin. It also was satisfactory for couples, so Julie was able to come periodically.

Effigy Mounds National Monument was established in 1949 and is located in northeastern Iowa, along the Mississippi River. Containing 2,526 acres, it was established to preserve 195 regularly constructed mounds, some in the shape of various animals, which were made by ancient native peoples. This park area also preserves forests, tall grass prairies, wetlands, and streams. My main jobs were to man the visitor center, provide EMS service, conduct interpretive hikes of a couple of hours each, and do an occasional trail patrol.

The monument represents an important link in a string of protected areas that preserve fish and wildlife areas encompassing hundreds of miles from Minnesota to Illinois. There is not much else to say in this section. Although I was available once again for EMS duty, there was, fortunately, nothing serious of note, in spite of the persistent hot and humid conditions encountered. Thus, this brings to an end the shortest chapter so far.

EFFIGY MOUNDS
NATIONAL MONUMENT

NATIONAL PARK SERVICE
UNITED STATES DEPARTMENT OF THE INTERIOR

← HEADQUARTERS — VISITOR CENTER

Panorama

Indian mounds along the trail

Little Bear Mound

Conical Mound

Hanging Rock & the Mississippi River

MT. RUSHMORE NATL. MEMORIAL – 2007

I WENT TO no park in 2006 since we were once again moving, but this time just from one part of town to another and becoming home owners rather than renters. In 2007, however, summer brought us back to the NPS at Mount Rushmore National Memorial and back to the Black Hills of South Dakota. Once again it was back to law enforcement. It had been 3 years since I had been a federal cop, and this was to prove a problem, but more on that later. I accepted this job because it was law enforcement which brought the enhanced pay, brought us back to the delightful Black Hills, and because we were offered the rare opportunity to have fully furnished married government housing.

Mount Rushmore is famous for the images of the 4 presidents carved out of granite on the side of this mountain. It has become not only a part of the NPS but also a national icon. The images of George Washington, Thomas Jefferson, Theodore Roosevelt, and Abraham Lincoln were the creation of sculptor Gutzon Borglum who worked on the project from 1927 until his death in 1941. Later that year, construction was ended due to lack of funds because of the demands of World War II. This park area encompasses 1,278 acres of evergreen forest in the heart of the Black Hills.

Even when I had worked law enforcement during the previous season, and preceded the current season with a standard 40-hour refresher, it still has taken me about 2 weeks to start thinking, observing, and acting like a cop again. I can't speak for anyone else, but that's the way it has been for me. In the 2007 season, however, it had been 3 years since I had worked in that capacity. This is the maximum allowed without losing the ability to be commissioned. To complicate matters further, I didn't receive a true LE refresher. It is difficult to get back into the swing of things simply by reading regulations and watching videos. A delay in all the red tape involved with my recommissioning made it too late to complete my hours any other way.

To complicate matters further, I had a temporary medical condition which, though not serious, was disconcerting and distracting. I did not comment on any of these issues to my superiors since I didn't want to appear to be alibiing for, what I considered to be, the worst performance I had ever had in the NPS. Fortunately, I was given no formal evaluation since my season did not encompass a full 90 days.

Another issue was the fact that we received intelligence that Rushmore was a potential terrorist target. This only made the high profile law enforcement even more pronounced - this at a time when I was coated with rust. An example of this still embarrasses me.

During the Sturgis Motorcycle Rally, we had reinforcements come in from other parks, and because there were plenty of motorcycle gangs in the area at that time, none of us patrolled alone. Also, during that week, we patrolled with different people each day. On one of these occasions, I ended up on a drug stop with 3 other rangers. The suspects turned out to be 2 cyclists - one man and one woman. My partner and I dealt with the woman and the other 2 with the man. The standard procedure in such a situation is for one officer to be the contact person and the other to cover the scene. Like in other situations that summer, I remembered this procedure after the situation was over. Instead, I acted as the second contact person, searching for drugs. Fortunately, the other contact ranger was much more vigilant than I was, so nothing bad happened.

We also had executive types from regional headquarters that seemed to have as much rust in terms of field work as me. I was paired up with a couple of them. In one case, we dealt with an illegal camping/campfire incident along the road, and my partner ended up treating these folks almost like common criminals, and I think that they hardly knew whether to laugh or cry. In my opinion, he raised the tension in a situation that was very routine. While working with another guy from region, we pulled over a semi-tractor trailer which was illegally operating as a commercial vehicle inside the boundaries of Mt. Rushmore. As I wrote the violation notice, my partner told me what collateral to write it for.

The amount he quoted me was $225.00. When I got back to HQ, I was chewed out by a supervisor for charging the wrong amount. I didn't tell this lady that it was one of HER bosses who had actually made the mistake (It was supposed to have been $275.00). Again, I didn't want to appear to be alibiing.

On the EMS front, there were a number of cases with the usual bumps and bruises. One case that I dealt with was not minor, however. It involved a gentleman who had fallen on a set of stairs on the Presidential Trail. When I got to the scene, I found him lying in a supine position on the steps, lying awkwardly with his feet on the upside and his head on the downside. He was fully conscious and, upon questioning him, found that he had a degenerative spinal condition. Thus, I decided that it was prudent not to try and move him at all, even from this awkward position, because of the possibility of further compromising his already compromised spine. We waited for ambulance personnel to arrive with a backboard and other spinal stabilization equipment so that he could be safely moved.

We had cases of headaches and dizziness which were perhaps related to summer heat, but one of these cases was more serious than usual. It occurred in the amphitheater during an evening program. I was called into the presence of a 58 year-old man who was suffering from dizziness, headache, and nausea. Since it had been a hot day, heat exhaustion was the first thing that came to mind. His situation was worse than usual, however, so I called for ranger Don Hart for assistance. The subject had chronic hypertension but no history of heart problems. Nevertheless, after we helped him into the air conditioned visitor center, he reclined on a bench. In the meantime, we gave him Gatorade and water to re-hydrate, and a bit later, he was placed on oxygen. Along with his wife, we kept observing him, and when he didn't seem to adequately recover, we recommended an ambulance and a trip to the hospital. It was a good thing too because it turned out that he was having a heart attack. It is best not to have tunnel vision when doing EMS work!

One other thing was disturbing about this incident. The visitor center has 2 levels, and we were on the lower one, needing to get the stretcher w/victim on to the elevator to get up to the walkway. Incredibly, some visitors, already on the elevator, were reluctant to give it up for the stricken man. With prodding they did, however. This incident indicates something that I have periodically noticed about people on vacation. They often act more self-centered than they normally would back home. I am not a psychologist, but I think that sometimes folks get so focused on "getting theirs" in terms of their recreation that they are reluctant to have anything interfere. I may be wrong, but that's the way I see it.

We had another heart attack situation that ended more tragically. A grandmother with grandchild in tow dropped dead on the walkway to the viewing area. I didn't get involved in this directly but arrived in time to direct foot traffic away from the scene.

The only other thing of note that summer involved the tremendous visitation on Independence Day and during the Sturgis Rally. We all took turns directing traffic, and I dealt with thousands of vehicles in that capacity. After hours of doing this, the bottom of one's feet just burn from standing on the hot pavement.

I will leave Mt. Rushmore by noting an odd cast of characters that we dealt with - a car full of deadbeats that had been eating the free breakfasts at motels that they didn't stay at. The most noteworthy things about them were their need for baths and a limited, but colorful, vocabulary! And so went the summer of 2007.

The 4 Presidents

Spangler at Rushmore

Avenue of Flags

The NPS crew plus reinforcements during the
Sturgis Motorcycle Rally - 2007

Wilson's Creek Natl. Battlefield - 2008

In 2008, it was off to Wilson's Creek National Battlefield, once again in the law enforcement division. I am a Civil War buff, so this was right up my alley. Wilson's Creek contains 1750 acres and was established in 1960. It is located in southwestern Missouri on the site of the first major Civil War battle west of the Mississippi River.

Although there was little employee housing, Julie and I found that there were many reasonably priced apartments available within easy commuting distance outside the park. The only problem was that they were not furnished. This forced us to be innovative. Since we had to bring everything from home in my little pickup truck, space was at a premium. Our answer was to fill the apartment with fold up and blow up furniture, including camp chairs, air mattress, and even a blowup couch!

Wilson's Creek will always be remembered as the place where my chronic battle with "mini-Obamacare" came to a head. A little background on this comment: When I first began with the Park Service, the required physicals were done in a very practical manner. The NPS decided what the fitness level needed to be in order to safely and efficiently do the required job. The NPS simply sent us the physical forms which indicated what needed to be checked out. We could then give the form to our family doctor- the one who knew our medical history best- in order to perform the required physical. Then I heard that, somewhere, an unfortunate NPS LE officer died of a heart attack, supposedly while chasing a suspect. He had slipped through the medical cracks. Those in the know are aware that there are rare medical conditions that may go unnoticed in any normal physical exam. As is often the case, the government overreacted.

The powers that be apparently no longer trusted local doctors to perform routine physicals. Thus, they decided to require perspective LE rangers to be examined by designated government physicians scattered around the country. I found myself sometimes needing to travel hundreds of miles, at my own expense just to use one of these 'chosen ones'. That wasn't the end of the problem, however. It appears that Uncle Sam didn't fully trust even these doctors. Therefore, all of these physical results from all over the country were sent to a single designated doctor stationed in Atlanta, Georgia for final approval - so a lot of data was filtered through an extremely small funnel. This, of course, meant extended delays in bringing personnel on board for the summer season (or, I assume, for winter seasonals also).

All of this had proved to be a problem for me long before Wilson's Creek. I had suffered a high frequency hearing loss in the Army stemming from gunfire on the shooting range, where I was acting as safety officer. Before the 2000 season at Wind Cave, I was at first denied passage of my physical. This was a surprise since the year before I had passed the hearing test with no problem and in 2000 I had tested out the same, or even slightly better. The rejection said that I might not be able to adequately do my job. This job was the same as the year before at the same place, and I had achieved another high performance rating. My supervisor contacted the medical people and informed them that I had proven the previous season that I had no problem fulfilling my duties. Their response was that they had no interest in what he had to say. After being sent for additional tests, and my writing a congressman in protest, they suddenly and mysteriously passed me.

By the time 2008 rolled around, they had apparently realized that the 'one-doctor approval system' didn't work, and they now had a panel of 'experts' to make the final determination. Surprisingly, my security background check had actually cleared in early May, but the physical approval was once again delayed. That clearance did not come until August. In the meantime, I once again acquired my 40 hours of LE refresher by video, research, etc. at Wilson's Creek, and once again I patrolled without weapons or commission for most of the summer. Finally, I was sent down to Buffalo National River in Arkansas on 5 August for my firearms qualification. After that, I was finally good to go.

While this delay had been going on, I was once again patrolling at night without weapons or a commission. This was much different than Ozark Scenic River, however. In this case, we closed the park at 2100, since there was no overnight camping. Also, unlike Ozark, this was a very low-volume crime area. In fact, this park area has an identity problem.

Although there are Civil War buffs that visit, it has become somewhat of a fitness training area for local folks. This is because the loop road through the park is a convenient 5 miles long with a convenient pedestrian strip along the edge. Thus many locals come to jog, walk, and bike while knowing exactly how far they are going. (There is, of course, nothing wrong with this.) While patrolling I could at least keep an eye on things, give verbal warnings for minor infractions (of which there were few), and deal with any medical issues. I also periodically was called upon to direct in traffic/parking situations, which, after Mt. Rushmore, was a piece of cake.

I was able to do building security checks during this time and made myself useful as the un-official EMS coordinator. I took the responsibility of ordering needed first aid and emergency equipment and updated first aid and jump kits, while I inventoried everything. I set up an EMS equipment checkout system and oriented the staff on it. Actual first aid incidents were rare, and though poison ivy and copperhead snakes were abundant, I don't recall a single case involving either.

Anyway, I was finally re-commissioned in early August and therefore, had a whole month in which to fully do my job, after all of the taxpayers' money spent for background checks and physicals, which I'm sure ran into the thousands of dollars! I did issue one citation after that for a vehicle left in the park overnight.

Before leaving 2008, I have to mention something about the folks at Wilson's Creek. A large number of them were conservative Christians, so I felt right at home. Everyone was friendly and helped in making me feel at home. It was a great bunch to work for and with!

The Ray House - A makeshift hospital during the battle.

Panorama

WILSON'S CREEK - 2009

FOR THE FIRST time since Wind Cave, we were headed back to the same park as the year before. We were also in the same apartment complex with the same 'blow-up' furniture, and this time we were able to get a first floor apartment. By the way, they had a swimming pool that I was once again able to do my swimming workouts in. Most of the same great people were in the park to work with. Unfortunately, the same big problem occurred - my physical. Now the government was micromanaging it even more so. They still had the approved facilities around the country, but now we were assigned to a particular one. I was assigned to one in a crime-ridden part of Chicago. What made this worse was that there was the possibility of having my eyes dilated, meaning my wife would have to go along to drive me home. No way was I going to take her in there. Thus, I put my foot down and called the medical contact people and explained my reasons for refusing to go in there. They said that they would relent just this once and let me go to my family doctor.

The physical saga was not over, however. Now, instead of one doctor in Atlanta evaluating the physicals, there was a panel of "experts" who were evaluating the completed physicals. At my hearing check, I routinely commented that some congestion (left over from a cold) might affect the tests. This was jotted down by the doctor. I passed the general physical with flying colors, including the spirometer test of lung capacity. Nevertheless, this was not good enough for the panel. They had noted the congestion comment and decided that the chest congestion, which I no longer had, required a four-part rehabilitation program before they would pass me.

My family doctor E-mailed the panel and told them in no uncertain terms that I did NOT have any lung problems. They had no interest in the opinion of the doctor who knew me best, medically speaking. I called and told the government spokesman that the congestion was over because my cold was over. I didn't need any rehabilitation. The robotic reply was that I would have to have the rehabilitation. I asked that my doctor be allowed to talk directly with this panel. The answer - no. I then asked if I could talk directly to them. The answer - maybe in a couple of weeks. This never happened! What were the medical qualifications of this spokesman? Who knows! Who was on the panel? Again, who knows!

I finally tried something as a last resort. I knew that rangers were sometimes given waivers for certain medical conditions. Thus, I asked for a waiver for my imaginary medical condition. The answer from the robotic spokesman - No! The reason - They could only give waivers for failed physicals, and they hadn't yet decided whether to fail me or not. This decision, to this day, has never come - government logic at its best!! Therefore, I spent the whole summer of 2009 without a commission and without the enhanced law enforcement pay. Unfortunately, the taxpayers did have to pay for my LE refresher training at Cuyahoga Valley National Park near Cleveland, Ohio. This training, of course, went for naught!

Even though I could not fully do the job that I was hired for, I did manage to make myself useful in the same way I did the previous season before commissioning. Once again, I served as unofficial EMS coordinator, provided security and did closing procedures, routine patrolling, and park closing procedures. I also patrolled all park trails and plotted their distances with a measuring wheel.

Before leaving 2009, I must not fail to relay another memorable Park Service experience. One day, chief ranger John Sutton asked me if I would like to get some overtime on a special assignment. I said fine, and was told it involved chaperoning some ghost hunters at the Ray House one evening at around midnight. The Ray House is one of the important stops along the road loop. In the mid-1800's it was the home of a farm family by that name. During and after the battle, it was used as a Confederate field hospital. A Confederate officer died there, and the body of commanding Union General Lyon was brought there after he was killed in the conflict. The house has been restored to look as nearly as possible as it did when the Ray family lived there.

This was such an unusual assignment, I invited my wife Julie to come along. My job was to make sure that nothing in the house was disturbed. I needn't have worried. These folks were not the superstitious nuts that I expected. They may have been a bit eccentric but appeared to be highly-educated and even somewhat scientific in their approach. They had some kind of hand held electronic devices that responded to electrical energy in the area, which they claimed indicated the presence of departed spirits. These devices responded like crazy inside the house, and they began speaking to the supposed spirits. Another activity was to use toys to entice the Ray children to appear and play with them, while speaking just like you would to little kids. At this point, Julie and I gave each other knowing looks! They had asked me if there was any electrical power sources on the premises that might affect their devices, and at the time I didn't know. (I did not know that there was electrical power operating in the basement.) In the middle of a dark house in the middle of the night, with all of these goings on, it was truly kind of spooky for my wife and me!

This was not the only place they checked out, however. They took their sensors in the area around the house and on some of the trails that wound their way through the battlefield. They seemed disappointed when Julie and I opted out of their trail search for ghost soldiers. We headed to the truck to chill out and wait for them to set up their trail cameras. Not expecting any spooks to show up, I asked them to let me see their film when they were developed. Rather, I was curious as to what wildlife was using our trails by night. They said O.K., but I never did get to see the tape.

I hope that my description of this event has not sounded too sarcastic because they really were nice polite folks. We didn't buy in to what they were doing but tried to remain respectful. After all, they were nice enough to give me a large Mountain Dew to keep awake and alert. (It didn't work!) Anyway, so much for 2009.

Wilson's Creek

Abundant wildflowers

Cannon firing demonstration

Yellowstone Natl. Park - 2113

In **2010, 2011,** and 2012 there was no Park Service for me. The struggle with the government physical the year before had been the last straw, and after 2011 I was no longer commissionable since you can't go more than 3 years without being commissioned - that is without starting from scratch and taking all of law enforcement school over again. I wasn't about to do that, especially at my age. This, of course, limited the job opportunities for me in the NPS. That wasn't the only complication. Married and family housing was scarce enough before, and permanent employees and LE personnel usually get first pick of those, so we found the pickings going from slim to none on housing. For this reason I reluctantly accepted an interpretation position at Yellowstone National Park since they did offer Julie and me a mobile home trailer to live in. Someone at church actually congratulated me on what he perceived as a 'step up' on the Park Service ladder. Many of us in the know, however, do not feel that way - too many people, too commercialized, and full of 'sidewalk' tourists on a high octane rat race. By that I mean very few visitors there ever leave the pavement (only 1%, so I hear). Many drive around, take pictures at the pull offs, buy souvenirs at the gift shops, visit Old Faithful and a few other notable stops and leave. Nevertheless, beggars can't be choosers, so I accepted.

Yellowstone was our first national park, established in 1872. It was one of only a handful of park areas that were established before the Park Service itself came into being in 1916. It also came into existence before there were park rangers. In those early days, the U.S. Army oversaw and protected the park. For a long time, it was the largest park area (until some of the Alaska parks were established). It is located mostly in northwestern Wyoming, but does bleed into Montana to the north and Idaho to the west. In spite of what I said above about crowds and commercialization, this is a marvelous resource!

Both Glacier and Yellowstone are rich in wildlife, but Yellowstone is a better wildlife viewing park because there are more open areas. Because it has well over 2 million acres, it is able to absorb the crowds well, and the commercialization, such as the large areas of pavement and parking lots at the Old Faithful Geyser, is misleading. Although there is excessive development near the roads, much of the backcountry is remote from most human activity. Glacier is a popular hiking and backpacking park, but this is much less so in Yellowstone.

So much for the background on the park itself. As to my own experience there in 2013, I can only say that it was surreal. The way that I can best describe it is the following. I was only there less than a week and this narrative will explain why. It is as accurate as I can recall except all names are changed, except for my wife and my own.

It was in March that I received a call from a lady supervisor in Yellowstone offering me an interpretation position with married housing. (From now on in this narrative I will refer to her as Susan Smith.) The conversation that followed was an ominous indication of things to come. After accepting this GS-5 position, I remarked that although some folks withdraw their acceptance after receiving better offers, I was a man of my word and would not do that. She sounded offended and remarked that women keep their word too. I answered that I was using the word 'man' generically. She then said that she didn't recognize that. She also said that she heard that I was too strict with visitors. I don't know where she got that information since it wasn't in any of my past performance evaluations. I assured her that this would not be a problem. In retrospect, I wish that I had quickly reconsidered my acceptance. In retrospect, I was too hasty in accepting the position. Julie and I should have prayed together before making the decision as we have at other times.

I left for Yellowstone on Tuesday, 7 May and arrived at my government quarters at Lake Village near Fishing Bridge in the early evening of Friday, 10 May. Julie was to follow later after her school teaching responsibilities were done. I had expected to find the park fully up and running, but this was not the case. I had only some venison sticks and trail mix for food and nothing was open close by to get more. There was also no hot water for a shower, and the refrigerator didn't seem to be working. Fortunately, a helpful maintenance man got the refrigerator going and another one got the hot water heater turned on the next day and pointed me to where I could fill my gas tank.

Meanwhile, 'back at the ranch', Julie was trying to get a temporary change of address set up at the post office. She didn't have a specific enough Yellowstone address for us, so while I was still on the road she E-mailed Susan Smith requesting it. During training the next week, Smith confronted me, in front of other employees, and said that she had given the information to Julie only because I wasn't there. She added that she normally did not deal with spouses and that it wouldn't happen again! I responded that we needed the information and that she (Smith) was our only contact at that time. She then walked away with no further comment.

During the course of that first week of orientation, a number of other incidents happened. First, we were sitting outside in a circle, about 10 of us, half from the Canyon group and the rest of us from the Lake sub-district. Smith preceded to chew me out for sitting next to the Canyon group rather than 10 feet away with the Lake group. She said that she had told us where to sit, but I hadn't heard her. Thinking that it was not a serious issue, I joked that my mistake was a family trait, in an effort to lighten the atmosphere. She remarked curtly that I needed to change that trait - so much for lightening the atmosphere!

During the course of the orientation instruction, the age of various geological structures and events in the area was discussed. Someone asked about visitors who believe that the Earth is only thousands of years old. We were told to say that all scientists support the facts that Yellowstone presents on the subject. I spoke up that all scientific 'facts' are potentially falsifiable and that there are a relatively small number of things that ALL scientists agree on, and perhaps it might be better to say 'most scientists' instead. As far as I could tell at the time, this comment was received in an acceptable manner.

As I was preparing my first program (on grizzly bears), Smith checked it over. I had written that grizzlies were a marvelous creation. She said that she was uncomfortable with the word 'creation'. I noted that I had not mentioned God and that unless the bears had existed forever, then they must have been created somehow. I indicated that, as a Christian, I believed that God was that Creator, but that I would not say that in my program. She said that she was still not comfortable with it since the word 'creation' has theological implications.

On Thursday of that first week of orientation, we were given a tour of the park. The tour ended at 1600 (4:00 PM) and I asked permission to go to nearby West Yellowstone to get a few groceries. I needed to get permission since we were still on the clock. After being lectured that I should 'manage my life better', Smith gave me permission.

There was another lady instructor at training, whose name I don't remember, who also appeared to have a giant chip on her shoulder. I had purchased a new digital watch shortly before leaving for Yellowstone and had no idea that the alarm was on because of my high frequency hearing loss. Unheard by me, it went off right in the middle of this gal's presentation and she went ballistic. I didn't even know how to turn it off when I found out what was happening. Someone next to me finally got it off. I explained my hearing problem, apologized and asked if she accepted the apology. She finally reluctantly answered yes in a loud voice.

This whole situation came to a head on the 5th day of orientation, Friday, 17 May. We were beginning computer orientation, and I was trying to set up a password to access E-mail, etc. The login was assigned by the park, and I selected the password as per park instructions. Everything went reasonably smooth at first, especially considering my lack of computer expertise, since the first computer accepted my information. Such was not the case at a second computer, however. This machine would not let me in. A long-time seasonal employee, John Doe, who had been patiently helping me, tried also, and no dice. Then Smith tried it with the same result. She then accused me of writing the password down wrong for her. (Earlier she had implied that I had misrepresented my computer skills on my application - this in front of other people.) I remarked that I didn't understand why I could get into one computer but not the other. She said that it was my fault and that the computer was smarter than me and didn't make mistakes - this also in front of other people.

At this point, she asked if I needed to talk to her alone. I said no. She then said to consider it an order. In private, she began to accuse me of misrepresenting my computer skills on my job application. I responded that a person at the application screening office in Harpers Ferry had advised me the year before that I needed to rate myself higher on the various skills. Nevertheless, Smith accused me of making excuses and said that I lied about my ability to use Power Point programs. I reminded her that the wording in the questionnaire asked about experience with Power Point OR slide programs. As a school teacher and park ranger, I have had years of experience preparing and presenting slide programs, but not Power Point. She said that I should have known that they meant only Power Point. I said that I answered the question the way that it was written. Incredibly, she replied yes, but I should have known what they really meant. This is textbook government logic and rationalization - communicate poorly and then blame the recipient for not figuring it out!

She then said that she hadn't wanted to hire me but had to because I was a veteran. I responded that I was a well-qualified ranger, as supported by my resume and the approximately 47 pages of support documents. In another incredible response, she said that she didn't have time to look at those things but had simply looked at my occupational questionnaire and checked with a "couple of people." Are you kidding me!? In the civilian world, a personnel officer who didn't bother to read the resume of an applicant wouldn't be employed long themselves!

Possibly the most puzzling thing of all to me was when she commented that she was uncomfortable with some of the things that she saw in me that week. I should have asked her what she was talking about, but was so surprised by that unexpected comment that I did not. We were mostly just taking notes and beginning to prepare our programs. (I have no idea what she meant - because I sat in the wrong place?, said I was a Christian?, used the word creation?, had my wife contact her?, or what....???)

I said that I would work extra hard to master the computer skills needed in the job, on my own time, if necessary. She said that no one would have time to help me. I said that perhaps I had better just leave then. (I also didn't fancy coming 1300 miles to be harassed for over 3 months!) She said that maybe I should consider it, but that I shouldn't decide until she returned at 4:30 PM from a meeting.

When I returned to the computer, John Doe calmly helped me solve the problem by simply changing the format of the login (The original was the one that the park had given me to use!). Then he changed one figure in the password - replacing the @ in it with a # symbol. I had not written it down wrong! Why the first computer had accepted the original information and the second computer had not - no one knew. Fortunately, I didn't hold my breath waiting for an apology from Smith, because it never came! Again, that is vintage government - screw up and cover it up by blaming someone else!

This all occurred before lunch on Friday. After Smith left, I told John that I believed that I would resign and leave. He asked me not to make that decision yet, but to go have a relaxing lunch and come back and talk to him at 1:00 PM. When we met again, John at first cautioned me not to make a decision while I was angry (good advice, by the way!). We sat down and analyzed out the situation. I mentioned that I had an unblemished Park Service record without a single bad performance rating, and didn't want an otherwise impressive resume left with a blemish at Yellowstone. I then asked John if he thought that I could be reasonably sure of not getting a bad one at Yellowstone from Smith. He could not give me any positive reinforcement on that. This pretty much settled things. John then called Smith and told her of my decision to resign. Considering our previous conversations, I was somewhat surprised that she seemed to be taken aback that I had decided to leave. I can't imagine why, since she had questioned my honesty and integrity, and had said she didn't want me there! We met at 4:30 PM, and I signed my resignation and walked out the door. One of the other new men followed me out and said that he didn't blame me for resigning, and might resign himself. I don't know whether he did or not. I packed up and left for home the next day. Thus ended the most bizarre experience that I have ever experienced in the National Park Service! So much for my personal experiences that are more fact than opinion.

The rest of this is my impression of some of the park policies that I found strange, and even bizarre. We were told to carry nothing in our pockets that might make noise or jingle (What, no car keys or pocket knife?!). We were told not to have bad breath, but nothing was mentioned about what to have in our first aid kits. Priorities!? We were told not to have anything on our belts except bear spray. (What, no micro shield CPR mask!?) No attempt was made to identify our first aid skills. No attempt was made to check physical fitness, or require a physical examination. The only concern was to be able to inspire and to impart information. Although our group included only those people hired as interpreters, the visitors do not normally make that kind of distinction. To them, we all wear the same uniform and have the same base skills.

We had a saying in Glacier. Always be prepared for the worst case scenario because, if you are ready for the worst, you can more easily adjust to a better situation. The reverse, of course, not so much. That is the problem with the extreme specialization of parks like Yellowstone. One young lady in our group who didn't look to be in very good physical condition commented that it would take her all day to hike only a couple of miles, and questioned whether she could make it at all. How could she possibly participate in a search in which all possible personnel are needed to be involved? What happens if there is a mass casualty event (e.g. a tour bus accident) requiring all available EMS resources, and at the same time a cardiac emergency with only a minimally trained (or less) interpreter available as a first responder. Our employers, the taxpaying public, have a right to expect us to be able to handle situations like this. We don't 'walk on water' like some folks mistakenly think, but we do need to be cross-trained in order to deal with the variety of situations that may come up. In fairness to Yellowstone, I don't believe that this situation is unique to this magnificent area. I hope and pray that it won't take a tragedy, for which the NPS is not prepared, to correct this situation.

So much for Yellowstone.

An important postscript: Most of the above Yellowstone narrative was included in a letter to my congressman. This resulted in a congressional inquiry by him. The response by Smith bore little similarity to what I wrote above. I suggested to Congressman Roskam's spokesman that both Smith and I take polygraph tests in regard to these events, but he said that this was not to be done. Thus, it was time for me to let go of this and walk away.

One last thing - a theological one. Sometimes when our ego gets the best of us, God takes us down a notch or two. In sorting out how this nightmare happened to me, I think that this may be at least part of it. Modesty forbids, but I have received almost universal praise for my NPS performances over the years. Whether justified or not, and it certainly wouldn't have been at Mt. Rushmore, this can be pretty heady stuff. My wife Julie, who knows me better than anyone, nailed it. Later, she said that she believed that I often applied to jobs that I really didn't want that much in order to hear my ego caressed by the hiring person. We all need to be humbled sometimes even if, as in this case, in an unjustified way. I can't help but think of the following Scripture:" But as for you, you meant evil against me; but God meant it for good…." (Genesis 50:20). Smith may not have known it, but she just may have been helping to give me a healthy dose of humility!

Yellowstone Scenes

Old Faithful Geyser

Grand Canyon of the Yellowstone

Bison calf

Bull Elk

PIPESTONE NATL. MONUMENT – 2014

IN 2014, IT was off to Pipestone National Monument. There was no NPS housing, but there is a college nearby, so there are local apartments available, and we were able to get one. It was not furnished so it was back to our fold up and inflatable furniture. I had wondered if I would be black-listed by the government for leaving Yellowstone so abruptly and prematurely. The superintendent there had assured Rep. Roskam that this would not be the case, but trusting government officials is not a hobby of mine. Nevertheless, in this case the assurance turned out to be true, since I received numerous inquiries of employment in 2014.

Nothing could have been more opposite between 2013 and 2014. Yellowstone is a large park - Pipestone is small (only 282 acres). Unlike Yellowstone, my supervisor here was a conservative Christian who was a youth leader at a local church. This is not a wildlife area, although there are some, of course. It was established in 1937 to preserve quarries where American Indians have historically obtained materials to make peace pipes and other items. Visitation is relatively light with bursts of activity during school field trips and tours. All of the folks here were friendly and easy to get along with, unlike at Yellowstone. To be fair, though, except for the two lady instructors, everyone at Yellowstone was helpful and friendly as well. The Pipestone people were particularly sensitive and helpful when we had a death in the family early in the summer. I was allowed to have as much time off as I needed, and the whole rest of the season, if necessary. Julie and I decided that I would honor my contract however, and so I took emergency leave and returned. Finally, in terms of the contrast between the two park areas, the length of the orientation training lasted only half a day, as opposed to two weeks at Yellowstone.

My duties at Pipestone were mainly confined to the visitor center since there were no regularly scheduled tours. I recall conducting one formal hike for park employees and had a few informal ones out on our short trail system. The main subject was rock or cliff succession. (This park area does have some of the best examples of this type of succession that I have seen.) I did receive a very complementary letter later from a college professor in California. It was nice to hear. I had another program ready on fire ecology but didn't have an opportunity to present it.

As the only EMT on hire, I did acquire that function also. Fortunately, I didn't have to deal with any serious illnesses or injuries, in spite of the fact that we had many elderly visitors - mostly heat-related and one minor ankle sprain. As I had done elsewhere, I inventoried the EMS supplies and rehabbed the first aid kits. I also set up an EMS supply system and a patient information sheet.

As to my daily interpretation duties, most of the time was spent in the visitor center manning the information desk, with a daily monitoring of the weather station and recording of pertinent meteorlogical data. I struggled with use of the computer as I always do.

This is as good a time as any to mention that all government employees are now required to take a computer security course within one week of coming on board. This made it seem so ludicrous to me when Hillary Clinton pleaded ignorance as to government computer security. I did design one bulletin board display showing an historical food chain in the area and also revised a couple of park brochures.

Ever the backcountry ranger, if only in spirit, I once again decided to compute trail distances - all 1.38 miles of the trail system. As at Wilson's Creek, I used a measuring wheel to compute the total distance as well as distances between the various viewpoints.

Well, that about covers my time at Pipestone National Monument. I was asked to come back by the superintendent, but there were just too many sad memories associated with the place in terms of our family tragedy. This was no fault of the park or its employees. They were fine to work with. This was just a matter of circumstance.

Pipestone National Monument

Quarries

Lake Hiawatha

Whitetail doe

Pipestone Creek

Winnewissa Falls

Lichen

MT. RAINIER NATL. PARK - 2115

2015 FOUND US headed for Mt. Rainier National Park in Washington, since I had accepted a GS-5 interp. position there. It was to run from 1 June to 7 September.

Mt. Rainier was the 5th park in the nation to be founded, being so designated in 1899. It contains 236,381 acres and centers around the massive 14,411 foot mountain of the same name. It has more than 25 glaciers on its slopes and is a favorite of mountain climbers. The mountain scenery here rivals that of Glacier and is a favorite of photographers. It is also a great area for wildlife, with deer, elk, mountain goats, black bears and mountain lions being some of the larger species.

I was able to accept this position because there was family housing available and direct train service from nearby Seattle to Chicago. Since Julie had to return early for school, this was a convenient connection. There was an aspect to this assignment that we had not known before. Since orientation was to last 2 weeks, and the training was to occur at Longmire, a long way from my permanent duty station at Ohanapecosh, it was necessary for us to live in a temporary location for the first 2 weeks and then move to our permanent summer residence. This, of course, meant an extra move was necessary. The first location was in a government apartment complex outside the regular park boundaries called Tahoma Woods. As seasonal housing goes, it wasn't too bad. The rub was - no phone service, land line or cellular and, at first, no internet or E-mail service. We were totally isolated from family communication. This was especially disconcerting since we were dealing with an illness in the family that we needed to monitor.

We drove 60 miles to finally get a cell phone signal and, fortunately, the internet began working later. Soon after that was worked out, however, it was time to move to my permanent duty station for the last part of orientation.

This permanent station is called Ohanapecosh. There was good news and bad news for us in this. The good news was that this is an impressive and beautiful area, in spite of the fact that it is the only developed area in the park where Mt. Rainier itself is not visible. The area is one of a thick evergreen forest containing old growth trees reaching 300' tall and 1000 years old. It is one of the most peaceful and least visited areas in the park as well, in spite of the fact that it contains a great trail system, an impressive campground, a river running through with the same name, and containing a waterfall to boot.

Now for the bad news. Our permanent quarters were considerably worse than our temporary ones had been. They were private in name only since the walls were apparently paper-thin. We could hear everything, and we do mean everything, in the apartment next door. To make matters worse, we had no communication with the outside world, unless we went into the little town of Packwood and used the pay phone at a gas station. This, of course, meant that no one could call us at all. We tried to get a land line with internet and satellite service, but the huge trees engulfing the area meant that a tall pole would have to be implanted in concrete outside our residence. I knew that, environmentally, the park wouldn't (and shouldn't) approve of that. This was all academic anyway since the cost to us would have been prohibitive. Thus the dye was cast! We would have to leave.

There was another issue that bothered me, although, considering the communication problem, it became irrelevant. At times, I was going to have to present programs to very young children. This had not been mentioned specifically in the original job description and application information from which I had decided to apply. I had no experience presenting programs exclusively to small children. To make matters worse, there didn't seem to be any guarantee that the parents would be with the children - making us glorified baby sitters! What if one of the kids decided to run off into the woods? Do we chase them and leave the others unsupervised? How much discipline and/or physical restraint were we allowed to exercise? This is a liability issue just waiting to happen! My advice to parents - always chaperone your children while in a park area (or anywhere else, for that matter)! My advice to the NPS - always insist that minors are supervised by their parents or guardians while in the park!

Thus, we packed up and left after only 3 weeks in the park. I was left with feelings of guilt and self-doubt. Had I explored all avenues in getting adequate affordable communication for us? I second-guessed myself about that. As an afterthought, should I have explored whether I might serve in another area of the park where we would have phone service in place? Worse, knowing beforehand that communication might be a problem, and remembering the family death we had experienced in 2014, why had I accepted the position in the first place? This was particularly selfish since we had another family member with serious ongoing health issues. As a Christian, I know that we are all selfish to some extent, but this was an example of my self-centeredness in spades! I just wanted that job!

I had also let the park down. I left them short-handed at the last minute, made worse by the fact that I was to have had an EMS function in the campground. Unlike Yellowstone, this was not a matter of being badly treated. As a matter of fact, they were very understanding and gracious over my abrupt resignation. They deserved better than what they got. Had I not selfishly accepted the position, someone else could have been hired who probably would have been available the whole season.

Julie had always wanted to visit Olympic National Park, and while we were that close, we took a side trip there. This was possible because the family illness that we were dealing with was serious, but chronic. Our need was not our immediate presence but our constant ability to communicate, so as long as we had phone access, we did not have to rush home. After what happened the year before, this was a high priority.

Olympic was a nice trip, and beyond just sight-seeing, we had a strange and interesting experience. While meeting one of the ranger supervisory personnel at a visitor center, I casually introduced myself, and startled, he called a cohort over with the comment, "Hey, this is Terry Spangler!" I didn't know how I had become a celebrity. I explained our situation and how we happened to be going home, and he remarked that they would be happy to hire me. He asked to talk to Julie, and when I got back to the truck she seemed down and depressed. I asked what the matter was, and she said that she now wondered if we should be going home. We talked about it, and I now believe that this was a test God was giving me. I was having my ego stroked once again. How would I react? Would I take the selfish route, or would I follow the 'me third' concept (God first, others second, and me third)? We decided to turn from my selfish ego and head home to deal with family obligations. I have certainly had my share of taking the wrong fork in the road, but, in this case, I believe we did the right thing.

Top & bottom pictures: Mt. Rainier
Middle: Elk, in a developed area just outside the park
boundary.

EPILOG

2013 BROUGHT THE disaster at Yellowstone; 2014 at Pipestone will be remembered for the death in the family; and 2015 at Mt. Rainier ended abruptly because of illness in the family. In 2016 and 2017 we stayed home because we couldn't find married housing anywhere. It seems that God is trying to grab my attention. I am sometimes dense and hard-headed, but feel that he is perhaps telling me to let go of that life and move on to other things. Another thing that has happened deals with a policy change in the NPS. All parks have been directed to provide restroom access accommodation to transgender individuals. One of the most common questions asked by visitors is: "Where is the rest room?" I could not imagine directing people to a RR that didn't match their sex. The Park Service will just have to initiate this policy without my help - just another indication that the Lord wants me out of all this!

My Park Service resume includes jobs at 15 different parks and training at 10 others. This includes work in 3 different divisions: interpretation, general, and law enforcement. In the process, I have formed some definite impressions about government employment. One impression can be illustrated by a staff meeting that I attended at Herbert Hoover. This was conducted by a person talking about liability and tort claims. We were told that as long as we were operating within the scope of our duties, the government would cover for us, even if we 'screwed up'. If I recall correctly, it was emphasized that the government had deep pockets and would shelter us in court. I sensed a bit of arrogance in this. It seemed to imply that we could perform poorly, and we would be immune from punishment. This wasn't said openly, just implied. It is my opinion that this tends to cause employees to not think outside the box. They cling to regulations for dear life like life preservers instead of using them as a tool. It can get to be very robotic.

Another observation/opinion deals with the term 'ranger'. In the military, a ranger may have a specific day-to-day job, but each one has a baseline skill set that identifies him as a ranger. There are expectations that he receive special training that all rangers must successfully complete to earn that label. Such is not the case in the NPS. The skill sets are as varied as the park areas that we work at. The job requirements are as different as night and day between a place like the Statue of Liberty and Glacier. Nevertheless, in both places the label is 'ranger'. To a certain extent this is understandable. The problem is that the people who pay our salaries, the tax-paying public, have certain expectations of all of us. There is an expectation, for example, that we are better prepared than the average Joe to deal with medical emergencies. They also associate us with outdoor skills and certain other traditional skills as well. When I was at Mt. Rushmore, a ranger executive said that I was part of a dying breed - 'an old-time ranger' (i.e. a 'jack of all trades, master of none'). Yes, the Park Service seems to have become more specialized since the days that we cross-trained at Glacier.

If it were up to me, I would make the following changes in order to guide the visitors' expectations. First, I would give the title 'ranger' only to those with the established ranger baseline skills. (A disclaimer: The picture pages herein that show traditional ranger skills are not meant to be all inclusive, but are simply examples of those skills that I happened to have pictures of!) Personnel without the baseline skills would acquire the title of 'technicians' that the biotechnicians already have. Hopefully, these changes would help better define the various roles of these divisions to the public. This is not to demean anyone. Interpreters, for instance, are the heart and soul of the NPS. These are the only park personnel that many visitors ever see. They are truly the frontline representatives of the NPS, and are, perhaps, the most indispensable of all. In Glacier, I had the privilege of working around such wonderful interpretive rangers as Dave Casteel, Clare Landry, and Bob Schuster. I just think that the services provided by the various divisions should be better defined to the public.

Another outstanding Glacier ranger and friend that I somehow managed not to mention enough in this narrative is Bob Isdahl.

He was also absent from all but one of the pictures. Nevertheless, he also has played an important role in my Park Service experience.

In terms of these divisions, I have made another observation over the years. There is a struggle among "LEOS" (law enforcement personnel) as to identity. Are they to be cops who happen to be rangers, or rangers who happen to operate as cops? Sometimes, I have seen obvious friction between those holding these opposing views. Depending on the park area and the administrators in charge at any particular time, there might be night and day differences in what would be expected of us. I know of at least one situation where patrol rangers were not thought to be doing their jobs unless they had issued at least one citation during each shift. (Pity the poor visitor who happened to run into a ranger near the end of his shift without having yet issued one!) At the other extreme, there are places where issuing any citations are discouraged. My philosophy has always been to issue them where needed, while hoping none are needed because everyone is behaving themselves. I have never been a "heat seeker" (i.e. LEOs who are always looking for excitement and action). Rather, I have often said, and believe, that the 3 most important aspects of the job are professionalism, professionalism, and professionalism. I have worked with a few heat seekers, but fortunately, they were in the great minority.

Finally, I would like to note that our park areas protect a large number of species that are susceptible to extinction. The endangered species issue is one that has always been near and dear to my heart. I have long been troubled by the apparent indifference to this issue by many fellow Christians. Many of them would be appalled if great man-created works of art were destroyed, and yet don't seem to be that concerned when the works of God (i.e. God-created species) are destroyed by man's activities. It is one thing to utilize the creations of nature and quite another to eliminate them completely.

In this regard, I noted an example at Glacier as to how difficult it is sometimes to determine the actual numbers of a given species in a given area. The estimated number of grizzlies present in the park when I was there was estimated to be between150 to 250. That's a very wide range, but for all of the time that I was out in the field with them, I couldn't have estimated a more precise figure. An accurate figure in Yellowstone was debated for years and was shrouded in controversy. A census on many other species is as difficult, or even more so, to attain - this in spite of the fact that species inevitably go on the endangered species list on the basis of numbers. Thus, as an afterthought, I have included my own possible solution to the issue (see appendix 3). That brings to an end my narrative of my Park Service experiences.

Glacier Rescue Training

Glacier rangers roped up-Grinnell Glacier.

Spangler, belaying off of an equalizing anchor and....

.... ascending out of a crevasse.

Mountain
Rescue
Training:

Mock rescue - packaging the "victim".

Regi Altop "on rapell".

Dave Casteel in the litter.

Mock rescue - carry out.

(The location of the two previous picture pages is Glacier Natl. Park.)

ACKNOWLEDGEMENTS

FIRST OF ALL, I would like to thank my long-suffering wife Julie, who I dragged around to all of these park areas, often to live in sub-standard housing in remote areas with few, if any, people to talk to. She also played an important role in preparing this manuscript. Without her help it wouldn't have been possible! Also, many of the uncredited pictures were taken by her and friends.

I would also like to thank my good friend Roger Shewmake for peeling my carcass off the side of a cliff. Without him, I likely would not be around to write this.

I also would like to give a shout-out to the technicians in the Glacier National Park library for laboriously copying and sending me the Many Glacier station logs for the five summers that I was there. Without them many incidents would have been forgotten and left out. Thanks also to a young college student, Steve Eivaz, who prepared the preliminary manuscript for publication.

When one starts to thank people for something, there is always a danger of leaving someone out. I will try to alleviate this possibility by saying that I am so grateful for all of the great friends that I have met in the NPS, including the ones that have always had my back.

Finally, I want to thank my parents, who introduced me to my Christian faith and helped nurture it; to my alma mater, Wheaton College who helped mature it; and, once again, my wife Julie, who has shared it with me.

One of the most photographed landscape scenes in the world-
Wild Goose Island in St. Mary Lake - Glacier National Park

1045: - GPI offices in East Glacier Whitefish Emily Mock -

1:00 - Mark Perry called the Grinnell System Main + Lobby will down until further notice ___ RB

1137 - They will be testing alarm system at Swiftcurrent for next 10 min

1145 - Regi to Grinnell Lake.

1203: 224 B radio check, ~~Father~~ Grinnell Lake -
×

1217 - Riddle Funeral home takes possession 3 M. Name withheld for privacy. 1217 to Browning MT.

1220 - Bear swimming outside of the bath- tub. Bear enjoying himself - Lee

310 Ken Pitt hiking up S.C. Pass via ~~Swiftcurrent~~ Valley

1320 524 x /and ? Hotel

1410 - We seem to have a light brown medium sized bear (possibly g bear) frequenting the Cracker Lake area - lots of tracks and scat on the

196

Appendix # 2

TRAIL LOG - TWO MEDICINE - 1986
(continued)

DATE	PERSONNEL	TRAIL DESTINATION	CONDITIONS	VISITOR CONTACT
July 7	516,517	Upper Two Medicine Lake Distance-9 mi. (canoe patrol-hike)	The purposes of this trip were: - to do a canoe patrol of 2 Med. L. and Pray Lake; - to clean and service the pit toilets at Upper Two Medicine Lake and the Pray Shelter; - to take pine oil to these two pit toilets; - to post signs warning people to lock the john doors after use; All of these things were accomplished. This was a mild, sunny and pleasantly relaxing day.	30 (approx.
July 10	516	Two Medicine Lake Loop Distance-8 mi.	This patrol was in response to an "overly-familiar" small black bear who apparently followed some people down the North Shore Trail for a ways yesterday at about 14:30 hrs.. I planned to be there at about the same time the next day to see if it showed up again. There was a freshly turned-over rock in the area but no other signs of the animal. Also, I mapped out in detail the 5 potential helicopter landing sites around the lake. See case/incident #860364.	30 (approx.
July 11	516	Two Medicine Lake Loop/ W. Aster Park	The purposes of this patrol were to check out bear sightings: on the North Shore Trail; along the South Shore Trail; along the Aster Park Trail. Except for fresh "bugging" rocks along the North Shore, I found nothing. Will we never see the end of rain, wind and snow?	9
July 12	516,517 317	Cobalt Lake Distance-11 mi.	The purposes of this patraol were: 1. To clean and service the pit toilet. 2. To paint the toilet seat. 3. To repair the door (fix hinges and door spring, etc.) 4. Post "please lock door" sign. #1, 2 and 4 were accomplished; #3 was temporarily accomplished, but the trail crew will need to repair the toilet	9

Appendix # 3

ENDANGERED SPECIES SUSCEPTIBILITY FACTORS

On my 10th birthday, very good friends gave me a book which has helped direct my life. I eagerly read and memorized it -'Wild Animals of the World' by William Bridges and Mary Baker. I virtually memorized all 268 pages! Later, as a high school biology teacher, I was searching for material to use in teaching about endangered species, one of my big passions. I was dismayed to find inadequate information on the subject so I decided to write a lesson from scratch based on my own background information. (This was in the late 1970s- early '80s.) In the process of preparing this lesson I examined the current US Fish & Wildlife list of endangered species. Harkening back to my remembrance of the above-mentioned book and other studies, I decided to go down the list and see what the various species had in common that might have contributed to their endangered status. I also wanted to compare them to other species that were common and resilient. As I looked at the various endangered species I tried to identify characteristics that they had in common that might have contributed to their endangered status. I identified 6 of these characteristics that I call 'extinction susceptibility factors'. I noted that each species on the list had at least one of these factors and I believe that these factors are cumulative (i.e. The more factors they have, the more susceptible they are). Please note that these factors were developed to apply only to vertebrate (higher) animals although some probably apply to some plants and invertebrates.

A little more background on this concerns how I found out that this list may not have been developed before. I was on a field trip with a group of my Pittsfield High School biology students to the Tyson Wolf Sanctuary just outside of St. Louis in the early 1980's. In the course of a conversation with the education director, we discussed the captive red wolves present at the sanctuary. I off-handedly rattled off the susceptibility factors that have caused this canid to become so critically endangered. He unexpectedly asked me what I was talking about and said that he had not heard of such a list being put together before. He asked me for a copy to put in their educational file. The realization that coordinating these characteristics might be new brought the desire to get the information authenticated by other biologists, particularly since I believed that the characteristics are cumulative (i.e. the more of these that the species has, the more susceptible they are).

The questions to be answered were the following:

1. Is the list valid?

2. If so, are there any additional characteristics that should be added to the list?

3. Are there any that should be subtracted from the list?

I ran the list past some of my Park Service collegues and the response was positive with no additions or corrections. While serving at Isle Royale National Park in 1985, I had the privilege of discussing this with Dr. Rolf Peterson, biology professor at Michigan Tech University, and one of the leading wolf experts in the world. He further discussed the list with a Swedish collegue and their response was similar, but with one caveat - they weren't sure that the list was valid for lower organisms (which I previously noted). I also discussed this with a biology professor from Western Illinois University who also gave a positive response and added that the information should be published. I was then invited to participate in a seminar at Western, teaching my material to area high school biology teachers.

Following is the list of 6 extinction susceptibility factors:

Low Reproductive Rate

Example: The grizzly bear sow reproduces only every third year and therefore this species does not recover quickly when their numbers are impacted. Contrast this to its cousin, the black bear sow, which reproduces every other year. Since the litter sizes of the two species are about the same (1-3 cubs per litter), the reproductive potential of the black bear is significantly greater than that of the grizzly. Therefore, the black bear population is more resilient and stable than that of the grizzly, particularly in the lower 48 states.

A Specific Food

A species existence can be no more stable than the stability of its food source(s). If the particular species eats a wide variety of foods, its population is much less likely to be compromised if one of these food sources becomes scarce or disappears. On the other hand, an animal that has only one food source that it depends on for survival will rise or fall with the availability of that particular food.

Example: The Everglades Kite is a medium-sized hawk that eats only the apple snail (although some individuals have rarely been known to eat fish and crayfish). With the draining of marshes in southern Florida, the apple snail has become much more rare and with it the kite, one of our most endangered birds.

Example: Contrast this to the raccoon which is an omnivore that eats almost anything. Eliminate mulberries (one of their favorite foods) and they simply eat other things. The raccoon is wide-ranging and abundant.

Intolerance To Man

If an animal species is intolerant to people or expanding human development, that species is likely to develop unstable and diminishing numbers. In many cases the reverse of this is also true (i.e. man's intolerance to it.).

Example: The Grey Wolf is one of the first animals to disappear when human development occurs in its habitat. Although the wolf adapts well to a wide variety of natural habitats, it doesn't do well around human development.

Example: Compare this to Canis lupus' smaller cousin, the coyote. This embattled fellow is much more tolerant of man than man is of him, and is one of the few large animals that has actually increased in numbers and range since the coming of European civilization.

A Specific Habitat

This factor is placed in the middle of the list because it is pivotal and most important and because all of the others are related to it. In fact, the key word in endangered species research is HABITAT since the habitat is the place where an organism lives and all of the limiting factors that make its life possible there. If a species can live in a wide variety of habitats (i.e. is very adaptable), there is much less of a chance that the population will be greatly impacted by the destruction of a specific habitat type.

Example: The Kirkland Warbler can live and reproduce not just in pine forests but only in Jack Pine forests and only among trees that are from 5-20 years old. Since Jack Pine trees reproduce only after fires, their life cycles have been interrupted by the efficiency of modern fire fighting and fire prevention techniques. Without fire to alter the timetable of forest succession, this transitional stage had been slowly disappearing and with it the Kirkland Warbler. Locked into a very specific transitional habitat, the little bird seemed doomed. Now, however, special areas have been preserved in Michigan where 'prescribed burns' are conducted assuring, at least for the time being, the continued existence of the immature Jack Pine forest and this little warbler that depends on it.

Example: In contrast, the coyote can be found above the timberline in the Rockies, in cornfields in the Midwest, or even in suburban areas. Whether desert or wetlands, these adaptable canids seem to thrive. As was stated previously, they have adapted so well to human development that they have actually increased in numbers and range. It is very unlikely that it could become extinct by habitat destruction since it seems to be able to live almost anywhere.

Tendency to Herd

Animals that live in close social contact with others of their kind may be more susceptible for several reasons: communicable diseases can spread more quickly through the population; natural occurrences such as fires, floods, or avalanches can destroy large populations at once; but the most significant reason is that the population is much more susceptible to human activities.

Example: The bison used to number in the millions on the North American Continent. In fact, perhaps 60,000,000 or more lived on the western plains as late as the first half of the 19th century. Then European settlers began killing them for food, sport, and profit. Living in large herds, they could be killed at a very high rate over a short period of time by riflemen, driven over cliffs by the hundreds, and many other ways. As trains passed through the thickly packed herds, "sportsmen" fired rifles as fast as they could load and reload. As long as they fired low enough they could hardly miss. By the beginning of the 20th Century the millions had become hundreds. Fortunately, under belated protection, the bison has now made a comeback. A solitary species would be much more difficult to kill at a rapid rate.

Example: The coyote is again the 'poster boy' for being the classic survivor. It is a mostly solitary animal (although it occasionally travels in small family groups). Whole packs of grey wolves can be killed by simply poisoning a partially-eaten kill- not normally so with coyotes.

Economic Value

If an animal species acquires a significant economic value (e.g. skin, fur, meat, horns, etc.), then it may become endangered regardless of whether it has any of the other factors or not.

Example: Alligator skins for leather have been coveted for a long time. This caused the alligator numbers to take a nose dive as poachers took a tremendous toll. Fortunately, alligators are now raised commercially on farms and that has greatly reduced the pressure on the wild population. Thus this species has dramatically recovered. This illustrates the fact that this is the most dynamic and changeable of the factors.

Example: Except for a brief period in the 1950s when there was a Davy Crockett coonskin cap fad, the body of the racoon holds nothing of any significant value and that was the only time (that I am aware of, anyway) that there was any significant decrease in numbers.

Proposed Uses of the 6 Extinction Susceptibility Factors

None of these factors are new or earth-shattering in themselves. Rather they are really just organized common sense. They are easy to perceive long before a species shows any signs of population instability. If an animal has any one of the factors it may go extinct and the more factors it has, the more likely that is to happen.

Organisms used to be classified in ascending levels of peril as rare, threatened, endangered, and, finally, extinct. These classifications have now been modified in ascending order of peril as follows: least concern, near-threatened, vulnerable, endangered, critically endangered, extinct in the wild, extinct. There is also another category that is actually based on a lack of enough data to make a determination as to actual status. All of the above categories rely heavily on knowledge or estimates of actual population numbers. This is fine when these numbers are easily obtained. Often this is not the case, however.

Several decades ago a controversy arose in Yellowstone National Park in regards to the health of the grizzly bear population there. It was very difficult to determine the actual numbers and whether those numbers were stable or not. I can personally sympathize with the problem. As a backcountry ranger in Glacier National Park in the 1980's, I hiked thousands of miles in grizzly country and was very much involved in bear management activities and yet I couldn't have given anything close to a definitive numbers figure. It was officially stated that there were estimated to be 150-250 grizzlies in the park. This is a very wide margin of error percentage-wise. Nevertheless, the park population is considered to be at carrying capacity.

Grizzly bears aren't the only species whose numbers are difficult to determine. Populations of species have gone extinct or nearly so while experts have debated the degree of peril. The premise of this discussion is that species should be classified with more of an emphasis on these 6 factors and less of an emphasis on perceived population numbers. The populations could be managed on the basis of these factors. Further, I believe that protective measures should be based specifically on the factor(s) that apply.

Example: If a species tends to live in large social groups and is a popular game species, set the bag limit significantly lower than for animals that may have similar numbers but live solitarily (since species that live in large groups can be killed at a more rapid rate). The same type of system could be used on the basis of species' reproductive rates. In some cases, they shouldn't be harvested at all.

Example: If a species has economic value, creating domestic sources of supply might very well take pressure off of the wild population as has already been successfully done with alligators and bison.

Example: Any habitat that is specific to a particular species should be aggressively preserved as is being done successfully with the Kirkland Warbler but was not done for the Ivory-billed Woodpecker.

Example: If a species relies almost exclusively on a particular food source, that food source should be protected at the same level as the species itself.

Example: If a species does not tolerate human development well, buffer areas should be created around their known home ranges in which human activity is significantly curtailed. This is probably the most difficult one to realize, politically speaking. The grizzly bear population in Glacier National Park is stable at least partly because there is very little development outside the park boundary on three sides. Large predators are particularly susceptible to human development in and around their home ranges because it requires large areas to support them.

In addition to the above uses of these factors, I believe that the level of jeopardy should be determined by the presence (or absence) of any of these factors and a permanent base level be established on the basis of the factor(s) that a particular species has (i.e. the more it has, the higher the level of protection). For instance, a species that has all six factors should permanently be protected as an endangered species even after perceived numbers rise into the 'safe' category. A species that has one of the factors should be listed no lower than 'vulnerable' with the option of a higher protective level as conditions dictate.

Summary

There is nothing new or different about any of these factors individually. That is the whole point - this information is usually easily known - much more easily known than numbers or numbers trends. They also can usually be known with much less financial expense involved. Although it would be politically difficult, I feel that a permanent baseline level of protection should be used based on the number of factors that each species has. Each organism should never be rated lower than their baseline category but could be raised to a higher critical level as circumstances might dictate. Finally, and, ideally, these measures should be amended into the Endangered Species Act of 1973.